RON DESANTIS

RON DESANTIS

BIOGRAPHY OF A NEW REPUBLICAN STRONGMAN

FLORE KAYL AND
LAURE PALLEZ

 FIRST HILL BOOKS

FIRST HILL BOOKS
An imprint of Wimbledon Publishing Company Limited (WPC)

This edition first published in UK and USA 2024
by FIRST HILL BOOKS
75–76 Blackfriars Road, London SE1 8HA, UK
or PO Box 9779, London SW19 7ZG, UK
and
244 Madison Ave #116, New York, NY 10016, USA

British Library Cataloging-in-Publication Data
A catalog record for this book is available from the British Library.

Library of Congress Control Number: 2024931214
A catalog record for this book has been requested.

ISBN-13: 978-1-83999-204-9 (Pbk)
ISBN-10: 1-83999-204-2 (Pbk)

Cover credit: Photos for Public Use - Governor Ron DeSantis

This title is also available as an e-book.

CONTENTS

INTRODUCTION

March 2020, the world holds its breath. The streets of major American cities and beyond are emptying. Stores and schools close. The word "lockdown" enters our daily vocabulary. We learn to work from home, making makeshift cloth masks so that we can shop in the few supermarkets and essential shops that remain open. The economy flounders, unemployment soars, and the managers of small and medium-sized businesses quickly suffer from the recession. We're under house arrest.

In early April 2020, Ron DeSantis, Florida's 46th governor, reluctantly orders a lockdown. Two weeks later, he assembles a team of close aides in his office and asks them to work on a plan to reopen Florida economy as quickly as possible and get his fellow citizens back to work. Finally, on May 5, 2020, a DeSantis executive order allows 64 of Florida's 67 counties to officially reopen their offices and businesses.

Strongly criticized in the national and international media, this decision, deemed imprudent and premature in the midst of the global Covid-19 pandemic, gives Ron DeSantis national—and even international—visibility for the first time. In fact, he is the first U.S. governor to stand up to the Centers for Disease Control and Prevention (CDC) and the influential Dr. Fauci, chief medical advisor to then U.S. president Donald Trump. Ron DeSantis receives a barrage of criticism from Democrats and the international community. But he receives at least as much praise from Republicans, and Donald Trump in particular. With this decision, both decried and applauded, DeSantis presents himself as the man who is freeing his state from the yoke of the CDC and the bureaucratic power of Washington. He moves to the forefront of the national media scene in the United States, entering the arena of the Republican Party's leading lights.

Ron DeSantis sees himself as the spearhead of first state freedom against central federal power and secondly of the fight against wokism. Wokism is a current of thought that claims to denounce what it considers to be all forms of injustice inflicted on sexual, ethnic, or religious minorities. The term has quickly become politicized, and Republicans are pointing out what they consider to be excesses. They often caricature Democrats as supporters of wokism, opening America's doors wide to migrants, encouraging the oversexualization of the civil society, and the loss of traditional family values. In a February 28, 2023 *Wall Street Journal* op-ed,[1] Ron DeSantis explains: "Woke ideology is a form of cultural Marxism," assuring that, "We are making Florida the state where the economy flourishes because we are the state where woke goes to die."

Since coming to power in Florida, he has implemented a battery of laws banning discussions of sexual orientation in schools up to high school. A staunch Republican, in 2023 he enacted laws allowing the unlicensed carrying of weapons in Florida and reducing the right to abortion to six weeks of pregnancy.

What's striking about DeSantis is his determination and the mechanics he puts in place within his administration. He uses all the powers at his disposal under the Florida constitution to unfold his political agenda, in every aspect of the administrative and civil lives of his fellow citizens.

According to one of our contacts within the DeSantis administration, Florida's governor has two stated goals for the future. The first is to focus on the growth of the *Sunshine State*, in which he develops and implements public policies that are often replicated by other states, such as Texas. Ron DeSantis's second declared objective: to fight with the Democrats and the Biden "regime," as he calls it.

Florida, the third most populous state in the United States with almost 22 million inhabitants, turned red in the 2022 national elections. In November of that year, Ron DeSantis was handily re-elected governor of Florida. Some Washington DC-based analysts saw DeSantis as the next president of the United States. He has many financial, religious, and lobbyist supporters. His youth and his influential wife bring a breath of fresh air to the American political scene. He stays away from pointless fights and is rather respectful of his former mentor Donald Trump, whom he keeps at a distance but rarely openly criticizes.

---

1 Ron DeSantis, Why I Stood up to Disney, *Wall Street Journal*, February 28, 2023.

Ever since Donald Trump declared his candidacy for the 2024 presidential elections, polls have shown DeSantis to be a serious contender. Even if the Trumpist base still prefers the original to the copy, a craze is building around the young Florida governor, who embodies a new generation of politicians.

Today, he is one of the best-known governors in Joe Biden's America. We are witnessing the emergence of a new Republican strongman.

PART 1

Ron DeSantis's Beginnings

CHAPTER 1

A BRILLIANT STUDENT

Ron DeSantis has always been a brilliant student. He was one of the top students at Our Lady of Lourdes Catholic School and then at Dunedin Public High School in Dunedin, a small suburb of Tampa on Florida's west coast. But what made him popular at the time was baseball. His team won the 1991 Little League World Series in the 10–12 age category. At the age of 12, Ron DeSantis was crowned city champion. It was perhaps at this time that he began to develop a taste for success and competition.

Born on September 14, 1978, in Jacksonville, Florida's largest city, Ronald Dion DeSantis, who goes by his father's first name, comes from a modest Italian family. His mother Karen, originally from Ohio, is a nurse, and his father Ron is a TV installer for Nielsen. He has a younger sister, Christina Marie, born in 1985, who died suddenly in 2015 in London of a pulmonary embolism.[1] Aged 30, she was a consultant with KPMG. The bereaved family and her fiancé have always remained discreetly silent about the circumstances of her death.

Ron DeSantis's first ancestor to set foot on American soil was his maternal great-great-grandfather, who arrived in Pennsylvania in 1904. In the generation that followed, his eight great-grandparents were Italian. His grassroots family heritage and relatively recent immigration to America set him apart from the major American and Republican political families and give him a certain middle-class credibility. Even today, DeSantis is quick to point out in his speeches that he comes from the middle class, a product of meritocracy. His modest origins have given him a kind of drive and a distrust of the establishment. It's one of the most characteristic traits of his personality.

---

1 Alexis Buisson, Ron DeSantis, de l'ambition et des mystères, *Tribune de Genève*, May 27, 2023.

DeSantis pursued an exemplary academic career: in 1997 he graduated from high school and was admitted on academic merit to the prestigious Yale in Connecticut. He majored in history and political science. One can only imagine the echo of his academic success in his family and high school, and more generally in his town. His father says to this day that this is what he is most proud of about his son.

At Yale, Ron joined the baseball team, becoming captain with an excellent track record. To help pay for his studies, which were very expensive and well beyond his parents' financial means, he took on a number of student jobs: sorting trash, valet parking, moving, coaching baseball for camps, and even working as an electrician's assistant on campus. Courageous, he worked during all his school vacations without respite. He often studied in the library. Between his jobs, studies, and baseball, this left him little time to get out and about.

Many Yale students come from wealthy families, and Ron DeSantis was not one of them. He occasionally attended parties but kept a low profile. He did, however, join the famous Delta Kappa Epsilon student fraternity. This student group is one of the oldest and most influential in the United States and counts among its former members both Presidents Bush, Supreme Court Justice Brett Kavanaugh, as well as numerous businessmen such as Howard Heinz and J.P. Morgan Junior. Former students remember him as cautious and ambitious.[2] According to one of his Delta Kappa Epsilon "brothers" at the time, DeSantis kept his distance from practices such as hazing new members or initiation ceremonies. He was already trying to protect his image and would leave when a situation displeased him. Even those who disliked him respected his intelligence. According to Gabriel Sherman's investigation for *Vanity Fair*,[3] Ron DeSantis was perceived as a brilliant, cold-blooded calculator.

In 2001, at the age of 22, DeSantis graduated *magna cum laude*.

---

2 Gabriel Sherman, Ron DeSantis, the Making and Remaking (and Remaking) of a MAGA Heir, *Vanity Fair*, September 27, 2022.
3 Ibid.

CHAPTER 2

DARLINGTON SCHOOL

DeSantis left Yale with $101 in his pocket, and one can imagine that the prospect of earning a living appealed to him. He took a gap year during which he worked as a history teacher and sports coach at the Darlington School in Georgia. This old-fashioned, chic school caters to boarders from Kindergarten to Senior year. According to former students,[1] DeSantis boasts that he is a graduate of Yale, and says loud and clear that this teaching job is just a short step in his career, and that he has a prestigious future ahead of him—perhaps even president of the United States one day!

He was generally well liked by students: confident and rather handsome, young girls liked him and young men looked up to him. He coached the baseball and soccer teams successfully and seemed to be generally well accepted. A few students mentioned that he often came to parties organized by his senior students. His presence as a teacher made some of them uncomfortable, but most didn't mind, as he was perceived as a cool 23-year-old teacher.

DeSantis would surely like to forget this period of his life during which, for once, he let his guard down and was less cautious than usual. In fact, that year spent in Georgia at Darlington School is summed up in a single line on his Wikipedia page and has simply disappeared from his official biography published in February 2023, *The Courage to Be Free*.[2] Despite efforts to make this experience disappear from his CV, it is a safe bet that his political enemies, whether Democrat or Republican, will not hesitate to retrieve any photos and use any testimony that could harm him in a future political campaign.

---

1 Frances Robles, Pranks, Parties and Politics: Ron DeSantis's Year as a Schoolteacher, *The New York Times*, November 17, 2022.
2 Ron DeSantis, The Courage to Be Free: Florida's Blueprint for America's Revival, Broadside Editions, *Harper Collins Publications*, March 2023.

Aside from his somewhat cantankerous attitude at the time, some students remember him for his polemical remarks on the Civil War.[3] Avoiding a direct defense of slavery, he nevertheless justified it on the grounds of economic necessity for landowners in the American South who needed labor. He had heated debates with his students during his lectures, and some of the African American students present have vivid, humiliating memories of them.

DeSantis often returned to this Civil War theme in his classes, to the point that in the middle of the year a group of students made a parody video of Professor DeSantis having his character declaim: "The Civil War was not about slavery! It was about two competing economic systems. One was in the North […] "[4] This light-hearted video is revealing of DeSantis's discourse at the time, in which we can already glimpse the vision of American history he would support later in his career.

Another telling anecdote: a former student at the Darlington School mentioned that, during one of his lectures, DeSantis expressed his intimate conviction that abortion was wrong. This remark, out of place in a teaching context, shocked many students at the time, who discussed it among themselves.

Between his positions on the Civil War and on abortion, we recognize traits of his current political discourse and of the anti-wokism culture war he champions today.

---

3 Frances Robles, Pranks, Parties and Politics: Ron DeSantis's Year as a Schoolteacher, *The New York Times*, November 17, 2022.
4 Frances Robles, Pranks, Parties and Politics: Ron DeSantis's Year as a Schoolteacher, *The New York Times*, November 17, 2022.

CHAPTER 3

HARVARD AND THE ARMY

In 2002, Ron DeSantis entered Harvard Law School in Massachusetts. In his second year, he was spotted by the U.S. Navy and began studying to become a Judge Advocate General (JAG), an elite corps of Navy lawyers. According to a friend at the time,[1] he was inspired by the Tom Cruise movie *A Few Good Men.* It is true that, at the time, there was a resemblance between the two men, who had the same brown hair and blue-green eyes.

In an interview on Fox News cable TV in February 2023 to mark the release of his autobiographical book, Ron DeSantis explains that his military involvement was motivated by the tragic terrorist attacks on the World Trade Center in New York and the Pentagon on September 11, 2001. As George W. Bush's America went to war against terrorism and sent troops to Iraq, Ron felt a moral obligation to join the army and contribute to the war effort. His grandfather had fought proudly in the Second World War, and it was important and logical for Ron to join the fight too.

In 2005, DeSantis graduated from Harvard with a Juris Doctor, and a diploma from the U.S. Navy's School of Justice. It was only logical that he should join the U.S. Navy. He was first stationed at the Mayport military base in Florida, and served as an attorney with the U.S. Navy's Office of South Asian Justice Affairs. His court cases involved drugs, sexual abuse, theft, fraud, and corruption. According to Gabriel Sherman, who interviewed several of his former Navy colleagues,[2] he earned a reputation for pride, considering

1 Dexter Filkins, Can Ron DeSantis Displace Donald Trump as the G.O.P.'s Combatant-in-chief, *The New Yorker,* June 27, 2022.
2 Gabriel Sherman, Ron DeSantis, the Making and Remaking (and Remaking) of a MAGA Heir, *Vanity Fair,* September 27, 2022.

his professional career to be a zero-sum game, that is, there can be no two winners, only one winner and one loser.

In 2006, he arrived at Joint Task Force Guantanamo (JTF-GTMO), working with detainees at the Guantanamo Bay detention camp. He was then promoted to lieutenant, and in 2007 volunteered to go to Iraq. He was sent to Coronado, California, the command center of the U.S. Navy, to join SEAL Team One. He was then deployed to Iraq and worked as a legal advisor to the Special Operations Command in Fallujah under Captain Dane Thorleifson. Lieutenant DeSantis's role was to ensure that Navy SEAL and Green Beret missions in the Euphrates Valley were conducted within the law. Prisoners of war must be interrogated and treated in compliance with international law and the Geneva Conventions, and that was particularly tense following the Abu Ghraib prison scandal.

In an interview with the *Miami Herald*,[3] Captain Thorleifson, who is a DeSantis supporter but has had no direct contact with him since that time, says of him: "He did a phenomenal job. […] It was a pretty complex time, with Iraqi sovereignty starting to take hold. I respected him a lot as a JAG (U.S. military acronym for Judge Advocate General). He was super smart, articulate, resourceful and a positive part of the staff. I relied on him heavily."

During Ron's mission in Iraq, a hundred Iraqis were arrested. Some were high-ranking military officers, others were rebels wearing suicide vests, and others were just ordinary civilians in the wrong place at the wrong time. It was DeSantis's responsibility to dispatch the detainees to the various legal entities of Iraq's nascent legal system.

In April 2008, he returned to the United States and joined the Naval Region Southeast Legal Service. Shortly afterward, the Department of Justice appointed him special assistant U.S. attorney at the U.S. Attorney Office in the middle district of Florida, which covers the justice operations of about a third of Florida. There, he prosecuted various offenders. At the same time, he continued to serve in the U.S. Navy until his honorable discharge from active duty in February 2010.

To this day, he remains a JAG reservist lieutenant. During his service, he was decorated on numerous occasions. The Bronze Star Medal, the Navy and Marine Corps Commendation Medal, the Global War on Terrorism Service Medal, and the Iraq Campaign Medal are among the decorations he received.

---

3 Emily L. Mahoney and Howard Altman, Ron DeSantis Touts his Military Records, but as a Lawyer what did he Do in Iraq?, *Miami Herald*, September 21, 2018.

His military experience was undeniably a personal success and enabled him to refine his future policy in the field of defense. In Iraq, he had a front-row seat to observe the difficulties and limits of American interventionist policy. To this day, DeSantis, like more and more Republicans in Washington, is against state interventionism and post-conflict nation-building. In this, and on many military-related issues, he is aligned with the classic positions of the Republican Party. When he later served in Congress in Washington, DeSantis always voted in favor of increases in the U.S. Defense budget and was heavily involved in supporting legislation giving greater authority to the Office of Veterans Affairs. He also joined the Foreign Affairs Committee and advocated for an improved U.S. anti-terrorism policy.

CHAPTER 4

CASEY DESANTIS

In 2006, as a young lawyer in the Navy, DeSantis was hitting balls on the driving range of the University of North Florida golf course. There, he met a beautiful young brunette with blue eyes who had also come to train alone. They struck up a conversation and quickly became inseparable. Three years later, in September 2009, Ron DeSantis and Casey Black got married at Orlando's Disney World Resort. Both Catholics, Ron was 32 at the time, Casey 30.

Shortly after their marriage, Ron left the Navy. Staying in the military would mean transferring every few years to a different military base, which the young couple did not want. Casey had a well-established career in Florida: she was a local celebrity as a TV presenter and investigative journalist. Ron did not want to go back to Iraq on deployment. He then took a job with a Jacksonville law firm and started writing his first book. More on that later.

Jill Casey Black grew up in Ohio, like Ron DeSantis's mother, and came from a middle-class family. Her father was an optometrist and her mother, of Sicilian descent, was a speech therapist at the elementary school where Casey and her sister were students. Like Ron, she had an exemplary academic and sporting record. She studied at the University of Charleston in South Carolina, graduating in 2003 with a degree in Economics and a minor in French. She is a member of their International Economics Honors Society. Casey is an accomplished equestrian: she is a three-time National Champion equestrian.

In September 2003, she left South Carolina and joined the modest local TV station WJXT based in Jacksonville, Florida. She worked there for around six years. Starting out as a reporter, she became the morning news anchor, then the evening news anchor, and finally a producer. In 2010, she produced coverage of the PGA golf tour. In 2011, she joined another local station to host her own talk show. She won an Emmy Award for her work as a presenter. She was nominated twice in the Production category—without winning—for her investigative work titled *Real Life CSI* and her documentary *Champion: The JT Townsend Story*, recounting the shattered life of an incredibly courageous young black Florida athlete following an accident.

January 20, 2009, Barack Obama formally became the 44th president of the United States. Over the next couple of years, Ron DeSantis grew increasingly shocked, according to him, by the *"leftist"* orientation of Obama's administration.[1] During this period, 2009–2010, Ron's political conscience awakened: he analyzed his past experiences, and after a naval career, he wanted to continue serving his country but in a different way.

From 2011, the young DeSantis couple focused on Ron's career, and in 2012 he ran for House representative in Washington representing Florida's 6th Congressional District. The ambitious Casey, who had been a member of the Republican Party of Florida since 2004, long before she met Ron, had strong Republican views and became his campaign manager. She introduced Ron to the wide network of wealthy and influential acquaintances she had built during her many years as a journalist. As a media professional, she trained him to succeed in his television appearances. However, Casey's greatest strength was to offer Ron a softer, rounder image. With the elegance of a Jackie Kennedy and the political strength of a Pat Nixon, Casey DeSantis led the campaign with a velvet glove and an iron fist.

In 2016, they welcomed their first child, a baby girl, Madison, followed by a baby boy, Mason, in 2018 and another baby girl, Mamie, in 2020.

---

1 Ron DeSantis, The Courage to Be Free: Florida's Blueprint for America's Revival, Broadside Editions, *Harper Collins Publications*, March 2023, page 37.

CHAPTER 5

DESANTIS AND THE FOUNDING FATHERS

"The powers delegated by the proposed Constitution to the Federal government are few and defined. Those which are to remain in the State governments are numerous and indefinite." In his autobiographical book, published in 2023,[1] DeSantis reminds us of the intentions of James Madison, one of the Founding Fathers, when he drafted the American Constitution at the end of the eighteenth century. The United States is a federation, and the states should enjoy a high degree of autonomy.

In 1995, Barack Obama published his biography entitled *Dreams from My Father: A Story of Race and Inheritance*. In it, he recounts his youth and his desire to change society.

In 2011, Ron DeSantis, still unknown in politics, published his first book entitled *Dreams from Our Founding Fathers: First Principles in the Age of Obama*. The title is no coincidence, of course, and he set out to dissect and oppose every one of the Obama administration's actions, which, in his view, were at odds with the intentions established by the Founding Fathers and the Constitution.

The premise of DeSantis's book is summed up in an adage that he recalls: "a government of laws and not of men." DeSantis is a scholar who loves the law. He believes that there is much wisdom in the American legal system as it is: far from being a set of obscure and archaic rules, as the progressive Barack Obama suggests in his book, DeSantis sees it as an objective and perennial legal framework that everyone must honor, and which guarantees the stability of American society and the respect for the rights of the American people. Also, Ron DeSantis asserts the legitimacy of each state to govern itself and

---

1 Ron DeSantis, The Courage to Be Free: Florida's Blueprint for America's Revival, Broadside Editions, *Harper Collins Publications*, March 2023, Page 146.

wants minimal interference from the central power in Washington. The book is highly technical and not easy reading for those who are not well-versed in American law. In fact, the 500-page book was far from a bestseller.

To recall the context of the period in which DeSantis wrote his book, one must recall the subprime crisis of September 2008, and the ensuing collapse of the American economy. Freshly elected president of the United States, Barack Obama signed an ambitious $787 billion Economic Stimulus Package for the American economy in February 2009, a continuation of the $700 billion bank bailout plan previously signed in October 2008 by the previous president, George W. Bush. Fiscal conservative Republicans like DeSantis at the time were outraged: they believed that the state should not intervene as much in the economy and considered Obama's bailout plan to be incoherent, chaotically implemented, and unchecked.

Shortly afterward, Obama continued to develop his program, supported by the majority in Congress led by Nancy Pelosi; and the Affordable Care Act known as Obamacare was passed in 2010. One of Obamacare's provisions requires employers with more than 50 employees to provide financial assistance for their employees to take out individual health insurance. If they refuse to comply, they are fined. With Obamacare, an additional 10 percent of the American population enjoys the benefits of health insurance coverage.[2]

The Affordable Care Act was perceived as scandalous for Republicans like DeSantis, who believe that there is nothing in the U.S. Constitution to indicate that one citizen (or entrepreneur) is obliged to pay for another person's healthcare. Unfortunately for them, the constitutional validity of Obamacare was upheld in June 2012 by the Supreme Court, arguing that Congress has the authority to impose the taxes it needs to carry out its policies.

---

2 Céline Jaeggy, Systèmes de santé : une comparaison France-États-Unis, *Fondation Jean-Jaurès*, May 15, 2023.

CHAPTER 6

THE RISE OF THE TEA PARTY

In his first book, DeSantis also recounts the rise of the Tea Party movement, which is no coincidence. Recall, the Tea Party is an American political movement born in 2009, a libertarian protest movement opposed to the growth of the federal state and its taxes. DeSantis's political line is a continuation of this political current which was dominant among Republicans from 2009 to 2016. Since 2016, the Tea Party has lost momentum as it was absorbed by "Trumpism" at the time of Donald Trump's 2016 presidential victory.

In February 2009, just a few days after the Economic Stimulus Package was signed into law, journalist Rick Santelli, editor-in-chief of CNBC Business News, vehemently opposed Obama's bailout plan, claiming in a speech to the Chicago Chamber of Commerce, Obama's hometown, that subsidies have a perverse effect: they will reward bad companies which have frivolous management, instead of supporting solid, serious companies which can withstand the crisis. He called for a return to the values of the Founding Fathers, who, according to him, would be shocked if they knew the extent to which the federal government now intervenes in the country's economic life. Santelli proposed organizing a Tea Party in Chicago a few months later. A simple journalist, he launched the Tea Party movement, perhaps without realizing its scope, which would soon be taken up by then-Alaska governor Sarah Palin.

Calling for a Tea Party is, of course, a direct reference to the Boston Tea Party, the political protest movement by American colonists against British hegemony in 1773. At the time, the colonists were protesting the heavy taxes imposed by Great Britain. The Boston Tea Party rallied all 13 American colonies to its cause and launched the War of Independence against Great Britain, which led to the independence of the United States in 1776. To refer to a Tea Party in 2009 is to encourage resistance against the federal government.

It also denies that the Economic Stimulus Package saved many companies from bankruptcy, thus preventing massive layoffs and violent economic depression.

As we can see, the Republicans attribute to the Founding Fathers' reservations about a strong federal government. However, we learn from the book *The Big Myth*[1] by Naomi Oreskes and Erik M. Conway, Harvard professors of the History of Science, that this is not the case. In fact, the Founding Fathers supported a framed and framing federal government, fair and always in the interest of the American people. But early 1900 a myth to the contrary was propagated by powerful organizations such as National Association of Manufacturers (NAM). This wealthy federation, which today includes the largest American companies (Pfizer, Johnson & Johnson, ExxonMobil, the American Steel conglomerate, etc.), was fighting against state intervention in its affairs since the nineteenth century. Corporate tax, the right to form a union, the right to demonstrate, the fight against child labor: any attempt to reform the state was quickly caricatured as progressive or even socialist, and above all as a hindrance to the success of the free market economy. Today, this line of thought has penetrated all strata of American society and is largely integrated into the political line of the Republican Party.

In short for the Tea Party: less government, less taxes. In the mid-term elections of November 2010, amid the recession that hit the United States, popular anger was on the rise. The Tea Party surfed on it and gained enough momentum to win 63 seats in the House of Representatives, won mainly over seasoned moderate Republicans. The Republican Party regained control of the House. DeSantis analyzed and learned a lot from this school of thought, both in terms of content and form, which would prove invaluable to him when it came to winning the next election two years later.

---

1 Naomi Oreskes and Erik Conway, The Big Myth: How American Business Taught Us to Loathe Government and Love the Free Market, *Bloomsbury Publishing*, February 2023.

CHAPTER 7

DESANTIS IN WASHINGTON

And so, in 2012, DeSantis embarked on the election campaign for a place in Congress as a representative based on the fundamental principles we have mentioned: less federal government intervention, more free economy and free enterprise, more fiscal responsibility too. Unbeknownst to the public at the time, he had only nine months to make a success of his gamble. Together with Casey, they divided up the streets of his constituency and embarked on a relentless door-to-door campaign. With Casey's notoriety, doors opened easily. At the same time and thanks to her network, Ron DeSantis managed to raise $1.1 million to finance his campaign, an impressive feat for a political newcomer. Ron DeSantis courted various political groups, including the influential and very conservative Club For Growth, which gave him $100,000.

In March 2012, Donald Trump tweeted about him:[1] "Iraq vet, Navy hero, Bronze Star, Yale, Harvard Law, running for Congress in Fla. Very impressive." Trump did not then have the influence he would later have, and this tweet may not have helped Ron DeSantis win. In any case, that happened, and DeSantis easily won the Republican primary and then, in November 2012, the general election against Democrat candidate Heather Beaven by a 15 percent margin. In his autobiography of 2023, he praised Casey's presence and support. The couple's intensive door-to-door canvassing paid off. "Nine months before, nobody gave us a chance. Now we were heading to the US House of Representatives,"[2] he says. The Ron-Casey team won its first victory.

In January 2013, the 34-year-old Ron DeSantis made his debut in Washington on the benches of the impressive House of Representatives.

---

1 @realdonaldtrump, Twitter, March 30, 2012.
2 Ron DeSantis, The Courage to Be Free: Florida's Blueprint for America's Revival, Broadside Editions, *Harper Collins Publications*, March 2023, page 44.

Obama had been re-elected for a second term. The House was still under Republican control, and the Senate remained Democrat.

He was one of the 435 representatives, and he took his role to heart: he was assiduous. He became a member of several committees including Judicial and Foreign Affairs. He was easily re-elected twice in 2014 and in 2016, until he decided to run for governor of Florida in 2018.

During his six years in the House of Representatives, DeSantis built relationships and worked on his political agenda. Casey stayed in Florida, where she worked and supported him as much as possible. During the week, Ron slept on the couch in his House office. He flew back to Florida every weekend.

From a middle-class background, he had little personal fortune when he arrived in Washington. He stood out from the other, generally wealthier, representatives in the House. Many former members of his team report that his mode of communication was brusque. Rather reserved by temperament, he only really trusted his wife. Both are said to be suspicious, and to avoid written communication whenever possible.[3] His mission was to denounce the privileged and affluent of Washington-DC, which he dubs "the DC swamp." He wanted to change Washington, rather than be part of it, and stay true to his Floridian roots as well as to the American Midwest to which he was—and is—very attached as both his mother and his wife are from Ohio.

He kept his cabinet's running costs to a minimum and fought against bureaucracy and establishment spending. He refused invitations to parties and cocktail parties organized by lobbies and think tanks to maintain his independence. In fact, shortly before his arrival in DC, he stopped all his stock-market transactions: he felt that too many representatives made attractive financial deals because they had inside information. He didn't want to be one of them.

He submitted several bills to limit the benefits offered to representatives and senators, such as the retirement pension allocated for life after only five years in the House. He also campaigned in favor of the non-accumulation of legislative mandates, which he considered contrary to the spirit of democracy intended by the Founding Fathers.

His seriousness and sincerity on these matters are to be commended. In his first month in office in Washington, he wrote a memorandum declaring

---

3 Gabriel Sherman, Ron DeSantis, the Making and Remaking (and Remaking) of a MAGA Heir, *Vanity Fair*, September 27, 2022.

that he would refuse to collect his own pension and all the health insurance benefits customarily offered to all representatives and senators, solely because all these benefits are paid for by the American taxpayer. This decision is perhaps commendable, but his sanctimonious tone did not sit well with Washington. A month later, he went one better, proposing legislation to freeze the salaries of all federal employees, including members of Congress from both chambers. Despite opposition from Nancy Pelosi, the bill passed the House of Representatives marking a first personal success for the young DeSantis. The bill stalled in the Senate.

His priority battle was of course to "stop Obama" and especially Obamacare, but there's only so much he could do at this stage of his career. He was also fighting against the power of federal agencies such as the FBI (Federal Bureau of Investigation), the CDC (Centers for Disease Control), or the powerful FDA (Food and Drugs Administration), already. By cutting their budgets, he believed it was possible to better control them and, above all, reduce their power to act.

The IRS (Internal Revenue Service) scandal in 2013 reinforced his conviction. In May 2013, several hundred Tea Party-affiliated associations demonstrated outside IRS offices across the United States. They protested the long and tedious examination of their files by IRS employees in charge of approval of their statutes and tax exemption status. Indeed, an association whose primary objective is the "welfare of the people" in the broadest sense can benefit from tax exemptions. It is also entitled, as a secondary purpose only, to fund political operations. Even if abuses do occur, the law must be the same for all associations of all political orientations, and DeSantis was quick to become the spokesman for conservative associations who were singled out for scrutiny.

In November 2013, before the House of Representatives, he spoke these words: "The power to tax is the power to destroy." After an official investigation, it became clear that there was indeed a political bias on the part of IRS employees against conservative PAC (Political Action Committee), and according to DeSantis, this could be likened to a form of obstruction of free speech. A few heads rolled in IRS management, and DeSantis emerged more convinced than ever that federal agencies were overstepping their bounds and politicizing to the left.

Among his other endeavors as a young congressman, DeSantis was also committed to veterans. Deeply affected by the suicide rate among veterans and the drug cocktails prescribed to them, he successfully fought to develop a program to allocate for therapy dogs to accompany veterans suffering from depression due to post-traumatic stress disorder. About economy, he refused to vote to raise the debt ceiling in 2013.[4] This exasperated some members of his own party. On two occasions, he also refused to vote in favor of increasing subsidies for the sugar industry, alienating Florida's powerful sugar lobby.

In 2017, Ron, accompanied by Casey and an official delegation, traveled to Jerusalem to identify a possible location for the new American embassy. Moving the American embassy in Israel from Tel Aviv to Jerusalem was a cause close to his heart because "Jerusalem was the eternal capital of the Jewish people,"[5] he says. Ron DeSantis pushed Donald Trump to keep his campaign promise to relocate the embassy and in May 2018, the new embassy in Jerusalem was inaugurated. Ron traveled there for the occasion as part of a very large American delegation led by Ivanka Trump and her husband Jared Kushner.

During his six years in Washington, DeSantis carved out a place for himself on the ultra-right wing of the Republicans. His intransigence on conservative values, his personal morality, and his financial austerity inspired trust and enabled him to enter the very closed circle of wealthy Republican donors such as the Koch family and Sheldon Adelson, who trusted him and financed him.

In 2022, his track record in Washington would also earn him Donald Trump's apt nickname of Ron "DeSanctimonius."

---

4 Ballotpedia, Ron DeSantis' Congressional History.

5 Ron DeSantis, The Courage to Be Free: Florida's Blueprint for America's Revival, Broadside Editions, *Harper Collins Publications,* March 2023, Page 60.

CHAPTER 8

THE FREEDOM CAUCUS

In each chamber of the U.S. Congress, senators and representatives can choose to belong to several informal interest and working groups called caucuses. It takes just two members to create a caucus, and an elected official can join as many caucuses as he or she wishes.

Caucuses are plentiful and often bipartisan and can cover any topic: political currents, scientific interests, security issues, societal questions. There is a caucus on blockchains, another on Afghanistan, one on breast cancer, and one on e-cigarettes, and another one on field hockey, and so on.

One of the best-known caucuses is the Freedom Caucus, which has been in the news a lot in recent years.[1] It was in 2014, in all discretion, that several conservatives supported by the then financially troubled Tea Party banded together to found the Freedom Caucus, which officially saw the light of day in 2015. The founding idea behind the creation of this caucus is that conservatives must become a real force of opposition to the Obama Administration. The Freedom Caucus supports two main principles: more fiscal responsibility (limits on federal spending) and less immigration (more border control and rejection of amnesty for illegal immigrants in the country). It bases its political action on the rejection of compromise with liberals in Congress, the rejection of Obamacare and, more generally, the rejection of Barack Obama's handling of the economic crisis facing the United States.

The Freedom Caucus traces its origins back to 1973. That year, to put pressure on the Republican leadership of the House of Representatives, which they considered too moderate, some 50 conservative Republicans banded together and founded the Republican Study Committee (RSC). This

---

1 Flore Kayl and Laure Pallez, Le "Freedom Caucus" du Congrès américain : origines et orientations, *Fondation Jean-Jaurès*, March 6, 2023.

conservative caucus mirrored at the time its contemporary counterpart, the Democrat Study Group, which was founded by progressive Democrats in 1959, and which had since become a powerful force in the House.

In the 2000s, the RSC became a majority party in the House, with around 150 representatives. In 2008, the financial crisis changed all that: discontent grew among the more conservative members of the RSC. They were unhappy with the tendency of some Republicans to collaborate with Democrats on bipartisan bills. At the same time, the Tea Party movement emerged in 2009, and in the years that followed, it structured itself to unite the right wing of the Republican Party.

In 2015, the Freedom Caucus was created by nine members including the young Ron DeSantis.[2] To become a member of this caucus, one has to be invited, and the leadership rotates. The group's first chairman was Ohio Congressman Jim Jordan. Today, the Freedom Caucus has around forty members.[3] Jim Jordan remains one of the most influential. When it comes to education, for example, the Ohio representative favors a very conservative agenda: he is one who opposes abortion and advocates the teaching of abstinence in schools.

By March–April 2016, as candidate Trump won one Republican primary after another in every state, the Freedom Caucus gradually dropped Candidate Ted Cruz, whom it had previously supported, and began backing Donald Trump. Ron DeSantis, as well as Jim Jordan, with whom he had become close, chose not to officially support anyone.[4] In November 2016, to the surprise of the Republican establishment, Donald Trump won the presidency of the United States against Hillary Clinton.

Between 2016 and 2020, the Freedom Caucus was rewarded for its early allegiance to the new president: many members attained high-level careers in the Trump administration, such that the caucus was seen as a career accelerator. According to Philip Wallach, a senior fellow at the Republican American Enterprise Institute (AEI) founded by Dick Cheney, that is what attracted some of the members. Others were more interested in becoming political celebrities than in influencing legislation in Congress. Some examples

---

2 Lauren French, 9 Republicans launch House Freedom caucus, *Politico*, January 26, 2015.

3 Drew Delsiver, Freedom Caucus Likely to Play a Bigger Role in New GOP-led House. So Who are they?, *Pew Research Center*, January 23, 2023.

4 Flore Kayl and Laure Pallez, Le "Freedom Caucus" du Congrès américain: origines et orientations, *Fondation Jean-Jaurès*, March 6, 2023.

are Congressman Matt Gaetz of Florida and Marjorie Taylor Greene of Georgia, who seem seduced by the media spotlight.

What does the Freedom Caucus stand for today? Less government interventionism, more deregulation, skepticism about the Biden Administration and military spending, skepticism about international development aid and the war in Ukraine. Tighter border controls and anti-immigration measures are also on the agenda.

One of the main levers the Freedom Caucus uses to influence Congressional legislative projects is to vote on bills separately and not as a bloc, even if these bills are authored by Republicans. In 2017, the Freedom Caucus members, showing they were not on Donald Trump's payroll, initially refused to vote for the Trump-backed healthcare bill that would have weakened Obamacare, a pet peeve of many conservative Republicans. They refused because they felt the bill did not go far enough and that moderate Republicans, at heart, did not really want to challenge Obamacare. The vote first failed in the House, but finally the Freedom Caucus rallied and passed the bill after intense negotiations. Despite all these efforts, the text was then rejected by the Republican-majority Senate. It was a real legislative failure for Donald Trump.[5] As we can see, when in power and like for any governing party, the Republican Party is not united and must deal with multiple factions to get legislation passed.

In January 2023, the Freedom Caucus showed the full extent of its influence at the opening of the first legislative session of the 118th Congress. Although more than half of its members and Donald Trump himself supported moderate Republican Kevin McCarthy for the post of Speaker, some twenty Republicans, mostly from the Freedom Caucus, refused to align with the party and vote for him. It took no less than 15 ballots for McCarthy to win, not only at the cost of major concessions to the Freedom Caucus, but also at the cost of weakening the Republican Party.

---

5 Michael Needham and Jacob Reses, How Republicans Stopped Pretending and Started Getting Real, *Politico*, May 16, 2017.

CHAPTER 9

2016, THE TRUMP YEAR

"November 8, 2016 was a day no American voter will ever forget."[1] During the night, Hillary Clinton called Donald Trump and conceded defeat in the presidential election. Trump's supporters were filled with immeasurable joy; Clinton's voters were filled with shock, despair, and rage. America was divided. Trump would have a considerable impact on the career of the young DeSantis.

Trump had already considered running for president on several occasions, in 1986 and 2000, and even in 2004, when he hosted his reality show *The Apprentice*. In 2015, when he launched himself as a presidential candidate, he could quite easily have joined the Democrat camp: he was a member of the Democrat Party for eight years from 2001 to 2009, claiming on CNN in 2004 that the economy was better off under a democrat government than under a republican one.[2] He also joined the Independent Party for a short while. But it was under the Republican banner that he finally ran in 2015, asserting during his campaign that he felt conservative in his way of being and in his way of life.

Perhaps this explains why his candidacy was not immediately taken seriously at first by many. Some analysts at the time even thought that his candidacy was a joke designed to sabotage the Republican primaries by siphoning votes from other candidates. Many Republicans, including Ron DeSantis according to *Vanity Fair* sources,[3] snickered.

But Donald Trump is a talented man, and it did not take long for him to become the talk of the town. His eloquence and charisma made him an ideal,

---

1 David Horowitz, Trump will Smash the Left and Win, *Editions Humanix Books*, 2020, page 1.
2 Chris Moody, Trump in '04: I Probably Identify More as a Democrat, *CNN*, July 22, 2015.
3 Gabriel Sherman, Ron DeSantis: The Making and Remaking (and Remaking) of a MAGA Heir, *Vanity Fair*, September 27, 2022.

warm-hearted figure who fired up the crowds. The polls completely missed his rise to power. And many will be wary of them in the future. The *New York Times* gave Clinton an 85 percent chance of victory.[4]

One of Donald Trump's stated campaign goals was to "drain the swamp," referring to the "muddy" political circles of Washington, DC. Trump promised to cleanse Washington of lobbyists and so-called political corruption. "I'm going to make government honest again," he wrote on Twitter in October 2016. On Twitter again, Trump addressed Americans directly, saying he wanted to turn power from Washington back to the people. These were the central themes of his 2016 presidential election campaign, along with that of building a wall on the US-Mexican border.

During his inauguration speech in January 2017, President Trump extolled the unity of the nation, but it had never been more divided than it would become under his presidency. Trump was quickly labeled a racist and white supremacist by his detractors. Added to this were accusations from the Democrat camp of incompetence, mental instability, and even dictatorship. Just a few days after his election, the anti-Trump resistance was organized around Democrat billionaire George Soros and numerous progressive philanthropists. Marches across the country were organized with slogans like "not my president."

As soon as he was inaugurated president of the United States, Donald Trump was attacked from all sides. Ron DeSantis, who had remained cautious and quiet during the election campaign, could not comprehend this: the attacks from the Democrats did not surprise him, even if they were extremely virulent, but those from the Republicans seemed to him unfair and out of place. He was distressed that the Republicans of the Washington establishment were not immediately seizing the opportunity of having a Republican president and a Republican-majority Congress to implement the major reforms he felt were necessary.

In 2017, the Mueller Special Counsel investigation into the alleged collusion of Donald Trump and his campaign teams with Russia was launched under a Republican House.[5] After two years of investigation and relentless media assaults against Trump, and at a cost to the American taxpayer estimated at $35 million, the Mueller team finally in 2019 produced the Mueller report which, despite regular proven contacts between Donald Trump's teams and the Russians, provided no evidence of such collusion.

---

4 Josh Katz, Who Will Be President?, *The New York Times*, November 8, 2016.
5 David Horowitz, Trump will Smash the Left and Win, *Humanix Books*, 2020.

In 2017 and 2018, DeSantis was one of the first Trump loyalists to go into battle to publicly defend Trump: he proposed legislation to cut funding for the Mueller investigation and accepted numerous TV interviews to defend Donald Trump against media "hysteria." This earned him lasting recognition from President Trump. In fact, he was invited on an official trip on the presidential Air Force One airplane in November 2017. A kind of virile friendship developed between the two men.

DeSantis was also disappointed by the lukewarmness of congressional Republicans; he believed that in 2017 the Republican Party had a golden opportunity to do great things and pass reforms. For him, voters were expecting change in Washington: 63 million voters expressed this at the ballot box by voting for Trump.

Unfortunately, DeSantis said, Republican—and Democrat—elites were holding back, and Congress was unable to find the funding to continue building the border wall. He noted that many politicians on the right and left, supported by lobbyists, were encouraging the mass regularization of illegal immigrants because America was sorely lacking in unskilled labor. Similarly, he noted the low motivation of Republicans in Congress to dismantle Obamacare, which in the meantime had become popular and was accepted by most voters. DeSantis then began to develop the rhetoric of the "uniparty" and to use the expression "DC swamp," a favorite of Donald Trump.

In the early years of the Trump presidency, we can find elements that would later be taken up by DeSantis. During the Trump administration, the economic priority was to put *America first* and to *Make America Great Again* (MAGA). Among other things, this meant relocating industries to the United States and moving them out of China, especially the most strategic ones. Trump's America was beginning to question the excesses of globalization and was deemphasizing any benefit that the United States derived from it such as cheap imported goods. Ultimately, it was each country's relationship with globalization that was being questioned: one needed to strive for greater independence, particularly an industrial one, to limit foreign interference in a country's economy and to strengthen democracy. The Covid-19 pandemic and the ensuing shortage of medicines, medical equipment, and everyday consumer goods proved the relevance of this analysis to the whole world. This line of thinking has grown among American elites, and we know now that this Trumpist international trade policy has been pursued by Biden since 2020. In fact, today most American politicians agree on a protectionist vision of the United States in the face of globalization, whatever their political persuasion. DeSantis is, of course, aligned with this US-centric position.

On immigration, DeSantis also agreed with Trump. Another theme of the Trump presidency that echoes DeSantis's positions was the questioning of "Identity Politics," exacerbated by the far-left of the Democrat camp. In Western democracies, the United States in particular, we are witnessing a social fragmentation that translates into political polarization.[6] Writer Christophe Guilluy tells us:[7] "The atomization of social movements and communitarianism are signs of the exhaustion of a model."

The litany of Donald Trump's failed impeachment on the basis of Russian interference brought to a close four eventful years of his Administration. DeSantis drew several lessons from these four years: first, populism appeals. As a brilliant middle-class intellectual, he recognized the need to build a persona with a heroic posture close to the people and the need for a simple, colloquial language. During the Trump presidency, he began using Trump's language tics and to appropriate his strong rhetoric. Second, Trump's irrationality and instability did him a disservice with the public and his supporters. DeSantis noted that he would have to avoid this pitfall, not in his nature anyway. Third, he understood the effectiveness and the power of a solid communication plan with well-thought-out slogans and a coherent and direct communication strategy via television and social networks.

---

6 Laure Pallez, Libéralisme économique et communautarisme font bon ménage, *Personal Blog*, June 18, 2020.

7 Christophe Guilluy, No Society, la fin de la classe moyenne occidentale, *Editions Flammarion*, 2018.

PART 2

Governor DeSantis

CHAPTER 10

2018, AN ELECTION ON THE LINE

In 2015, Marco Rubio, one of Florida's two senators, launched his presidential campaign bid and announced he was vacating his Senate seat: DeSantis, then just one of Florida's 28 representatives in the House in Washington, threw himself into the campaign to reclaim this prestigious seat. However, Donald Trump defied all odds to win back the Republican Party's nomination in the 2016 Florida Republican primary, under the nose of Marco Rubio. Rubio then wanted to reclaim his Senate seat. DeSantis had no choice but to withdraw from the Senate race. He easily won reelection as a House representative in November 2016, but he was getting impatient.

Since Trump came to power in January 2017, we saw that DeSantis was disappointed in the Washington Republicans. Moreover, in the fall of 2017, his wife Casey, who still lived in Florida, became pregnant with their second child. Ron then decided not to seek a fourth term as a representative in Washington. In 2018, he turned his focus to Florida and entered the gubernatorial race.

He started with a fairly low baseline in the polls and lacked name recognition, but his strength laid in his ability to raise funds, which he did throughout his campaign. His main Republican competitor was Adam Putnam, Florida's state agriculture commissioner, a moderate Republican backed by, among others, the sugar industry lobby. At the start of the campaign, DeSantis was in trouble, with Putnam leading with a comfortable 17 percent lead. DeSantis then used to his advantage the close relationship he had cultivated with the all-powerful President Donald Trump. He launched a campaign spot underlining his political alignment with Trump (more on this later), and on more than two occasions Donald Trump publicly endorsed him. He was able to surge ahead of his Republican rival and DeSantis won the Florida primary. But there was more to come: he now needed to face the Democrat candidate, Andrew Gillum, in the general election.

In American society, economic issues are often perceived as being better managed by Republicans than by Democrats. While the biggest deficits in the American budget were made by Republicans George W. Bush and Donald Trump, 48 percent of voters put their trust in Republicans on the topic of the economy, compared to only 36 percent in Democrats in 2022.[1] Now Florida had been experiencing demographic and economic growth for over 15 years. From 2010 to 2018, this economic prosperity benefited the previous governor, Republican Rick Scott. Ron DeSantis hoped to benefit too.

Yet, no sooner had DeSantis been nominated as the official candidate of the Republican Party in August 2018 than he committed a faux pas. While being interviewed by a Fox News reporter, he declared, "The last thing we need to do is to monkey this up by trying to embrace a socialist agenda with huge tax increases and bankrupting the state," referring to his Democrat opponent. The expression *to monkey this up* means to make a mess of things, but the term "monkey" is particularly out of place given that Andrew Gillum is an African American and was running to become Florida's first black governor. The media pounced on DeSantis, who denied having meant to insult his competitor. Despite his denials, the shadow of racism hung over his campaign, and in September 2018, less than six weeks before the general election, he was trailing in the polls behind Andrew Gillum.

That was when Trump came to his rescue and advised him to hire Susie Wiles, Trump's previous campaign manager. A shadowy woman with the physique of a charming grandmother, Susie Wiles helped Trump win Florida in 2016 thanks to her impressive experience in lobbying and politics. DeSantis, urged on by Florida Republican Party executives worried by his lackluster performance, recognized that he needed Trumps' help and hired Wiles.

In November 2018, thanks to the support of Donald Trump, Susie Wiles, and wealthy donors, DeSantis finally won the election with 49.6 percent of the vote (4,076,000 votes), a meager 30,000-vote lead over his opponent (49.2 percent with 4,044,000 votes). A recount was even necessary. It was a hard-fought victory, but a victory nonetheless.

At 40, Ron DeSantis became Florida's 46th governor.

---

1 Morning Consult/Politico poll of 1,004 People Conducted July 15–17, 2022.

CHAPTER 11

GOVERNOR DESANTIS'S FIRST STEPS

Ron DeSantis took office in January 2019 and got to work immediately. By this time, he was a protégé of Donald Trump and continued to use him to his advantage. In the fall of 2019, DeSantis forced Trump's hand to come as a special guest to his annual state dinner in Florida. Trump accepted and showed his support. Yet, DeSantis slowly distanced himself from the Trump Administration: in 2019 DeSantis did only three interviews on Fox News, down from 81 interviews in 2018, a decision taken perhaps to avoid having to defend Trump's erratic and controversial record.

One of the decisions that sheds light on how DeSantis would gradually distance himself from Trump came in September 2019, when the *Tampa Bay Times* published an article highlighting the very particular fundraising campaign of Susie Wiles, his ex-campaign manager handpicked by Donald Trump:[1] the political action committee she then headed on behalf of Ron DeSantis wanted to charge $25,000 to anyone willing to play golf with the governor. DeSantis was furious that the information had leaked to the press, and according to the *New York Times*[2] he fired Susie Wiles on the spot, Donald Trump's close ally, attempting to sully her reputation with the Republican lobbyists and politicians both in Florida and in Washington.

Back to State affairs: in 2019, the young governor DeSantis enacted legislation focused primarily on the organization of state affairs. In the wake of the 2018 Parkland, FL high school massacre, which left 17 dead including 14 students, DeSantis was intractable with Sheriff Scott Israel, who had badly

---

1 Matt Flegenheimer, Maggie Haberman and Michael C. Bender, DeSantis Tried to Bury Her. Now She's Helping Trump Try to Bury Him, *The New York Times*, April 18, 2023.

2 Ibid.

mismanaged law enforcement at the high school: DeSantis fired the Sheriff as soon as he took office. He also held the leaders of the county's school academy accountable, and they were also dismissed. However, he remained at odds with the gun restrictions put in place by the previous governorship, because he considered the Second Amendment of the Constitution to be a higher principle and an inalienable right. He extended the authorization to carry firearms to teachers in the classroom. All schools already had an armed guard at the entrance, usually personnel drawn from the police force. From now on, this guard could train those teachers who wanted to carry weapons.

Another important piece of legislation for him was the Family Empowerment Scholarship Act. True to his commitment to parents' freedom to choose their children's education, he signed a law giving less-fortunate children the same opportunities to access private schools as children from wealthier families. The law offered children from working-class backgrounds the opportunity to attend any school they wish, be it public, charter, private, or even to be home-schooled, and provided for part of the tuition fees drawing on taxpayers' money even if their choice was to opt for a private school. This law was generally well received and was passed with a bipartisan majority vote.

At the same time, Casey DeSantis, as First Lady of Florida, launched several programs in the early years of her husband's governorship. HOPE Florida is a partnership with the Adecco group, which helps Floridians who dropped out of the workforce to find a job. RESILIENCE Florida combats the stigma associated with mental health problems and is supported by American football player Tom Brady. CHARACTER Education Standards is a charter that defines the values of resilience, responsibility, and respect in State Education and was adopted by the State Board of Education in July 2021. Casey DeSantis also launched THE FACTS, YOUR FUTURE campaign to combat drug use.

But her most personal and important commitment was her campaign against breast cancer. In 2021, Casey DeSantis was diagnosed with the disease. At 41, she was the mother of three young children. The family remained discreet about this intimate battle, but in February 2022, Ron DeSantis announced that she was out of the woods and in remission. In a campaign advert in 2022, Casey DeSantis reflected publicly about this difficult period, underlining Ron's supportiveness in her struggle. Since then, she has become very involved, visiting patients in hospitals, and promoting work to encourage early detection of breast cancer.

CHAPTER 12

COVID-19 AND EMANCIPATION

Let's flashback to 2020, a pivotal year in Ron DeSantis's career: by managing the Covid-19 pandemic he really found his own style and broke free from other politicians. He became a role model for other Republican governors and gained prominence and a nationwide reputation in the process.

At first, in March 2020, DeSantis agreed to follow the CDC response plan to Covid-19 called "15 Days to Slow the Spread." He agreed to the lockdowns, the school closings, and the use of masks. However, he could not understand the rationale behind sending Covid-positive patients from hospitals back to nursing homes where they could not be seen to medically, so he ordered retirement homes to adopt a policy of total isolation and he prohibited hospitals from discharging Covid-positive patients. Florida was one of the first states to set up Covid-19 testing centers and to order masks for all medical personnel. During this period, DeSantis often appeared in public with a mask. However, what were supposed to be temporary measures to slow the spread of Covid-19 became step by step a permanent shutdown. And that, DeSantis refused to accept.[1]

By the end of April 2020, DeSantis lifted one confinement measure after another. He sympathized with Florida's middle class who did not have enough savings to survive without working for even a few weeks, and with the working class for whom remote working was simply not an option, and with the plight of restaurateurs and small and medium-sized business owners. But the number of Covid-19 cases in Florida was exploding.

During this period in spring 2020, DeSantis immersed himself in the medical literature and began to harbor growing doubts about the scientific

---

1 Ron DeSantis, The Courage to Be Free: Florida's Blueprint for America's Revival, Broadside Editions, *Harper Collins Publications*, March 2023, Page 159.

experts' opinions as propounded by Washington. He contacted several medical authorities to find out more about Covid-19 and ended up reading Professor Jay Bhattacharya, a controversial epidemiologist and economist at Stanford University, who denied the effectiveness of masks in combating Covid-19 transmission. Masks would prevent droplets from circulating, he thought, but the virus would circulate in clouds, which a standard or makeshift mask could not obstruct. According to the professor, only a properly worn medical mask could prevent contamination. At the same time, and in view of the upsurge in cases, the mayor of Miami ordered masks to be worn in public and imposed heavy fines for non-compliance. The number of cases in Miami-Dade County dropped drastically.

DeSantis saw this initiative by the mayor of Miami as an unacceptable infringement of individual freedom, and in September 2020 he lifted all regulations imposing the use of masks. He issued a decree prohibiting any local jurisdiction, school districts, or city hall, from imposing the use of masks. That month, Florida recorded over 100,000 new cases, and hospitals were overwhelmed. As a preventive measure, DeSantis asked the federal government for equipment (respirators), which he obtained.[2]

In August 2020, Floridian schools reopened, offering parents the option of sending their children to school or not. However, some school districts continued to impose the mask mandate on pupils, which was a policy in opposition to the governor's decree. The penalty for ignoring the governor's decree was the non-payment of the school board members' salaries. Washington intervened and offset this with an exceptional federal grant, enabling board members to receive an amount equivalent to their usual salaries.

Later, once vaccination for kids was available, another decree forbade public schools from asking teachers or students about their vaccination status. However, in Miami-Dade County, the largest school district in Florida, a very large majority of the population over the age of 12 had a complete vaccination record. Beyond physical health, students' mental health was a priority. We spoke with Élodie, a teacher in Fort Myers, who explained that the mental health of her students deteriorated during the Covid-19 pandemic: it was already pretty bad before the pandemic due to peer harassment and social media addictions,[3] and it became even more serious because of Covid-19.

---

2 Timothy Bella, Florida to Receive Hundreds of Ventilators from U.S. Government to Help State's Record Hospitalizations, *The Washington Post*, August 11, 2021.

3 Laure Pallez, Elodie, professeure à Fort Myers, FL, *Personal Blog*, April 2020.

Another sensitive subject where DeSantis was not sure at first which stance to take: the vaccine, that Trump promoted and on which he was basing his future re-election in the November 2020 presidential elections. At first, DeSantis seemed convinced of the vaccine's effectiveness. He focused on deployment of the vaccine and then on injection of second doses to the most vulnerable senior populations.

In January 2021, after Trump's election defeat and Biden's victory, DeSantis replied abruptly to CNN journalist Rosa Flores, who insistently asked him why the vaccination campaign in Florida was so chaotic. DeSantis said: "There are a lot of requests. [...] How many questions are you going to ask me? Do you have three? The other journalists only have one each, so why do you have three?" In the end, he explained more calmly that most hospitals had adopted a relatively sensible first-come, first-served policy, but he came out of this tense exchange even more convinced than ever not to accept any more questions from "corporate media" journalists. Indeed, he was regularly attacked by mainstream media, with some even nicknaming him Ron Death-Santis. After this, he turned to Fox News, which aired a seven-minute documentary about the 1,000,000th senior Floridian who had been vaccinated. The sunny, light-hearted report aired on January 22, 2021. DeSantis's collaboration with Fox News then intensified.

In April 2021, Ron DeSantis himself received the Johnson & Johnson vaccine. Then he quickly changed his tune. Sensing that popular opinion was turning and that part of the Republican electorate had grown hostile to the vaccine, he forbade companies from requiring their employees to be vaccinated. In September 2021, at a press conference, he did not contradict a municipal employee when the latter, upset with the municipality of Gainesville, FL, which required its municipal workers to be vaccinated, declared that the vaccine modified RNA. At the end of September 2021, DeSantis appointed Joseph Ladapo as Florida's General Surgeon. This appointment was highly controversial:[4] Joseph Ladapo, who holds a Harvard degree in medicine and has taught at the prestigious New York University, has made numerous statements questioning the effectiveness of lockdown, masking, and vaccination in the fight against Covid-19. He has also promoted hydroxychloroquine, the anti-malaria drug banned by the FDA for use in cases of Covid-19.

---

4 Arek Sarkissian, How a Doctor Who Questioned Vaccine Safety Became DeSantis' Surgeon General Pick, *Politico*, October 1, 2021.

In November 2021, DeSantis banned all local decrees related to mandatory vaccination. He refused to answer reporters' questions about whether he had received his booster shot, claiming his right to privacy and asserting the information could be used against him politically. Donald Trump has not been shy about declaring that those who refuse to say whether they have received the vaccine booster are cowards. Tensions were running high between the two men.

Nationally, the United States recorded over a million deaths from Covid-19 in a total population of around 332 millions. Despite all the restrictions there, the highest death toll was recorded in California (99,000). Texas was next (at 90,000), followed by Florida (with 85,000) and New York (which had 76,000 deaths). Politically, it is difficult for the Democrats to establish a direct link between the health policies implemented during the pandemic and the number of deaths per state. Additionally, some political figures who implemented draconian anti-Covid-19 public policies in their own states came to Florida on vacation during the pandemic. At the end of December 2021, New York Democrat Alexandria Ocasio-Cortez was photographed without a mask at a party in Miami. Ron DeSantis sent her a now-famous ironic tweet:[5] "Welcome to Florida, AOC! We hope you're enjoying a taste of freedom here in the Sunshine State thanks to @RonDeSantisFL's leadership." According to Ron DeSantis, politicians of all stripes have done the same, and he denounced their hypocrisy.[6]

During a TV debate in October 2022, when DeSantis was running for re-election, his Democrat opponent Charlie Crist attacked him on this issue, estimating that more than 40,000 people could have avoided death from Covid-19 in Florida if lockdowns and the use of masks had been more firmly imposed. Ultimately, this attack would have no impact on the outcome of the election as DeSantis won re-election on November 8, 2022, with a 20 percent lead over Charlie Crist.

In December 2022, Ron DeSantis asked the Florida Supreme Court of Justice to investigate all vaccine advocates, from CDC executives to President Biden, to uncover any bribes or collusion between them and the pharmaceutical companies that produced the vaccines. This calculated outing enabled him to capitalize on his anti-vaccine image and to flirt once again with the Republican

---

5 @TeamDeSantis, Twitter, December 30, 2021.
6 Alexandria Ocasio-Cortez Under Fire for "Fleeing" to Florida Amid Lockdown in Home State of New York, *The Telegraph*, January 4, 2022.

electoral base on this subject before the pandemic would be fading to no more than a bad memory.

On March 7, 2023, DeSantis posted a letter on his Twitter (now X) account addressed to President Joe Biden asking him to allow Novak Djokovic to enter the United States to take part in the Miami Open tennis tournament. Since the start of the pandemic, the United States required all foreigners wishing to enter the country to be vaccinated, and Djokovic was not. The tournament started a few days later, and the unvaccinated headliner was not allowed to participate. As DeSantis pointed out in his letter, it seemed absurd that this rule should still be applied, even though Joe Biden declared in September 2022 that "the pandemic is over." It would not be until May 2023 that the Biden administration would announce the end of the requirement that international travelers show proof of their Covid-19 vaccinations.

CHAPTER 13

COMMUNICATION STRATEGY

Fox News is a key element of DeSantis's public relations campaign. He refuses to waste his time with other TV channels. Instead, he focuses on his electorate, and his voters watch Fox News. Nowadays, he only talks within a conservative media bubble.

He has a long-standing aversion to the "corporate" media, which he describes as leftist. In his autobiography,[1] he recounted how, in 2017, a left-wing extremist shot at members of the Republican congressional team during their baseball practice in Alexandria, Virginia. DeSantis remembered the moment vividly because he narrowly escaped the shooting. Congressman Steve Scalise (R) was wounded. The attacker was a supporter of Bernie Sanders, the leader of the progressive left wing, and the attack was politically motivated. The shooter hated Donald Trump, and "his goal was to massacre as many Republicans as possible," related DeSantis, who noted that at the time, major newspapers never mentioned the link between Bernie Sanders, his anti-Trump rhetoric, and the assailant. DeSantis had no doubt that the narrative would have been different had the attacker been from the far-right and the victims Democrats.

And so, progressively, DeSantis developed a distrust of corporate media. In July 2022, he banned journalists from the *New York Times*, *Washington Post*, and *Politico* from attending the annual GOP Sunshine Summit in Florida. At a conference in Pittsburg,[2] he declared:

> Look at what the corporate media does to advance these phony narratives. They know Biden's not doing a good job. So, what do they try to do? They

---

1 Ron DeSantis, The Courage to be Free: Florida's Blueprint for America's Revival, Broadside Editions, *Harper Collins Publications*, March 2023, page 71.
2 Gabriel Sherman, Ron DeSantis, the Making and Remaking (and Remaking) of a MAGA Heir, *Vanity Fair*, September 27, 2022.

try to concoct a blizzard of lies to try to get people not to recognize the failures of his leadership. And they do it day after day. And they lie day after day.

More generally, DeSantis believes he does not need Independents or Democrats to win and to govern, and that is actually a Trump-inspired strategy. Do not try to appeal to Democrat voters, consolidate your base and make sure all Republican voters, even those who reject civil society and never vote, turn out to vote that day. This strategy is a well-known winning strategy.

In fact, beyond this strategy, DeSantis adopted elements of Trump's rhetoric, for example when he speaks of the Biden "regime" to describe the Biden Administration. He told presenter Guy Benson in an interview on Fox News Radio in March 2022: "The contrast between a doddering, quasi-senile president who has to have his press team clean up his remarks after every time he opens his mouth, versus somebody like me who's out there—I'm very direct, I mean what I say, I lead, and I get things done."[3] Aggressive remarks and overconfidence are typical attributes of a Trump-like posture.

In 2018, when he was embroiled in the very close election campaign for the Republican primary nomination for governor of Florida, he paid homage to Trump in a campaign spot.[4] We see him encouraging his little daughter to play with plastic bricks and build a wall, an obvious reference to the wall along the U.S. border with Mexico. Then he reads Donald Trump's book *The Art of the Deal* to his three-year-old son: "Then Mr. Trump said: 'You're fired!' I love that part!" Faced with the ridiculousness of the scene and the criticism of journalists, his wife Casey later maintained that this campaign spot was obviously not to be taken at face value. Fair enough, but the main message— that voting DeSantis was tantamount to voting Trump—came across perfectly to Republican voters in Florida in 2018. And with this ad, DeSantis also gained notoriety. Obviously, it worked, as we know he won the Republican primary by more than a 20 percent margin over his rival.

---

3 Interview by Guy Benson, DeSantis: Florida, Not "Doddering, Quasi-Senile" Biden, Is Leading The Country And Free World, *Fox News Radio*, March 29, 2022.
4 Ron DeSantis ad Children MAGA, *YouTube*, July 30, 2018.

DeSantis followed Fox News polls very closely: he adapted each of his appearances to them. To members of his team, he would ask before each appearance, "How will that play on Fox?"[5]

His wife Casey, a seasoned television professional, taught him the ropes. Very involved in shaping his image, she taught him how to use a teleprompter, to look into the camera to address viewers directly, and she even chose the earpiece and microphone he uses. She made him wear a pair of cowboy boots because that would be more in keeping with the style of his constituents. Florida's Republican congressman in Washington Matt Gaetz told Politico reporter Michael Kruze in 2021: "I learned how to do my makeup *[for a TV set]* from Ron DeSantis, and he learned from Casey."[6]

Between 2017 and 2021, DeSantis was a frequent contributor to Fox News. Following the events of the Capitol Hill attack on January 6, 2021, he became temporarily more discreet. Moreover, he never went along with Donald Trump's rhetoric that the November 2020 elections were rigged. Instead, and more in line with his character, he kept a demeanor of calm and a cautious reserve.

Mid-2021, Fox News needed a new leading luminary as an alternative to Trump to occupy the evening news and daily talk shows. The network closed in on Ron DeSantis. Every time he appeared on television, Fox News' ratings went up. There was a real desire on Fox's part to make him a national figure. Numerous email exchanges between show producers and Ron's team prove just how close the collaboration was. According to an article published in the *New Yorker*[7] in June 2022, the producers of Fox News shows approached him and his team at least 110 times in 2021 to offer appearances, and he accepted at least 34 times. Fox News promoted Ron DeSantis's libertarian management of the Covid-19 pandemic. DeSantis's team could suggest topics, and even steer debates as they saw fit. DeSantis himself communicated by text with Sean Hannity and Laura Ingraham, the channel's two star-presenters. The machine was oiled: DeSantis fed off of Fox' polls, and Fox fed off of DeSantis's

---

5 Gabriel Sherman, Ron DeSantis, the Making and Remaking (and Remaking) of a MAGA Heir, *Vanity Fair*, September 27, 2022.

6 Michael Kruse, The Casey DeSantis Problem: "His Greatest Asset and His Greatest Liability," *Politico*, May 19, 2023.

7 Dexter Filkins, Can Ron DeSantis displace Donald Trump as the G.O.P.'s Combatant-in-Chief?, *The New Yorker*, June 27, 2022.

popularity. Since 2017, he has made no fewer than 200 appearances on Fox News.

In addition to Fox News, DeSantis enjoyed the support of *Florida's Voice* and *Florida Standard,* two digital newspapers that were born when he took office in 2019 and are run by close friends. The DeSantis Administration regularly provided them with scoops,[8] forcing other media outlets to follow suit.

DeSantis also relies on X (formerly Twitter), and on his communications director, Christina Pushaw. A true conservative pit bull, Pushaw says out loud what the notable DeSantis cannot always say. In 2021, Christina Pushaw was 30 years old and worked for a charity founded by the Koch brothers, two billionaires from an industrial family of Republicans who supported DeSantis. On her own initiative, Pushaw published articles on Republican blogs defending DeSantis's policies in an aggressive tone. She also led an online harassment campaign against a Florida nurse who said she was fired because she refused to downplay her hospital's reported Covid-19 caseload. Pushaw applied for a job in DeSantis's press office and, in view of her accomplishments and enthusiasm, he quickly hired her.

According to the *Tampa Bay Times*, Pushaw published over 3,000 tweets in her first six weeks in the job. She became the one who could say anything, from false claims to the vilest harassments. In fact, her Twitter account was suspended for 12 hours in August 2021 after she sent out 200 tweets in less than 24 hours against an Associated Press reporter, setting the web ablaze and generating serious online threats against the journalist. During the debate on the Don't Say Gay Act, to which we will return later, she accused all those who opposed the law of being pedophiles. DeSantis was satisfied with her work, and in August 2022 she was promoted to his campaign team during his reelection campaign for governor.

Around that same time Ron DeSantis, then leading in all the polls, unveiled a new facet of his communication strategy. He became Top Gov. The campaign spot[9] was humorously inspired by the latest *Top Gun* film. Set in the "Freedom Headquarters," the video features DeSantis and his son at the controls of a jet, both wearing leather jackets and aviator sunglasses. Their mission: to fight corporate media. Clearly, DeSantis's admiration for Tom Cruise covers decades.

---

8 Molly Ball, The DeSantis Project, *Time Magazine*, May 18, 2023.
9 Top Gov Ron DeSantis, *YouTube*, August 23, 2022.

CHAPTER 14

DESANTIS'S TOOLBOX

Under Florida law, a governor can only serve two consecutive terms of four years each. Once elected in 2018, Ron DeSantis had only eight years at best ahead of him to fulfill his vision for Florida. We already saw what kind of laws and decrees he implemented in the first years of his governorship up until COVID. The political success he achieved thanks to his management of Covid-19 reinforced his strategy. Supported by a Florida Congress devoted to his cause, he passed a battery of conservative laws between 2020 and 2022 regulating many aspects of the cultural and social life of Florida citizens.

How did he implement this strategy? DeSantis is pragmatic and motivated. In January 2019, having just taken office as governor, DeSantis asked his cabinet to present him with an exhaustive list of all the constitutional, executive, judicial, and nominative powers now vested in him. He was determined to use every legal lever at his disposal to achieve his conservative goals.

The Florida Congress is made up of a 40-member Senate and a 120-member House of Representatives. Representatives to the House are elected every two years for a maximum of four terms. Senators, on the other hand, are elected every four years for a maximum of two terms. As in many states, Florida's two legislative bodies do not sit year-round at the Capitol in Tallahassee, Florida's capital, but only for 60 days a year. Exceptional sessions can be called, if necessary, outside these 60 days.

Following the November 2018 elections in Florida, the Senate was made up of 23 Republicans and 17 Democrats. By November 2022, it had increased up to 28 Republicans and 12 Democrats. Same scenario in the House of Representatives: Republicans had a clear majority in 2022, with 78 Republicans versus 42 Democrats. DeSantis was therefore the leader of a state in which Republicans had a large majority in the Senate, the House of Representatives, and of course he was at the head of the executive branch. This *trifecta* means power is concentrated in the hands of a single party.

DeSantis thus had a free hand to unfold his agenda, and this was all the truer as Florida could be characterized as *trifecta plus*. Indeed, the Florida Supreme Court is also predominantly conservative, giving the 4th power, Judicial, to the Republican Party. The function of the Florida Supreme Court is to be the last judicial resort for all matters concerning Florida. It is composed of six justices and a chief justice. Judges are appointed by the governor for six-year terms, while the chief justice is elected. Currently, five of the six justices have been appointed by DeSantis since he became governor in 2018. Unlike the federal Supreme Court, for which the justices are appointed for life by the president of the United States, the Florida Supreme Court is therefore likely to be partisan, especially as the governor before DeSantis, Rick Scott, was also a Republican and had also appointed conservative justices. This judicial power is powerful in confirming or overturning legislative decisions that go against or in favor of DeSantis's plans. The most blatant example of this partisanship is gerrymandering of the electoral map, as explained by journalist Gary Fineout for Politico.[1]

Every ten years, following the decennial federal census, states are allowed to revise their electoral maps. Officially, they must take account of population changes, but they often take advantage of this review to redraw electoral districts to suit their political stripe. Gerrymandering is not exclusive to Republicans; Democrats are no strangers to it either. But Ludivine Gilli, an historian specialized in the United States, asserts it is more common in Republican-controlled states.[2] The aim of GOP (Grand Old Party, nickname of the Republican Party) gerrymandering is to break up electoral districts where Democrats systematically win elections by solid margins and dilute them in other districts with strong Republican majorities. These districts can be very close to each other geographically, making gerrymandering easier.

But in Florida, there is a law dating from 2010 entitled Florida's Fair Districts, the aim of which is precisely to prohibit gerrymandering and to protect the votes of minorities, and particularly African Americans—who vote overwhelmingly Democrat. The law was passed by referendum in 2010 and incorporated into the Florida Constitution.

Following the 2020 census, the Florida Congress reworked a reasonable electoral map that complied with the Fair Districts Act. They presented it to

---

1 Gary Fineout, Florida Supreme Court Locks in DeSantis-Backed Redistricting Map, *Politico*, June 2, 2022.

2 Ludivine Gilli, La révolution conservatrice aux Etats-Unis, Editions de l'Aube, 2022.

Ron DeSantis, who, to everyone's surprise, vetoed it. He then redrew the map to his liking, dividing Florida into 28 new districts, 20 of which went to the Republicans and only 8 to the Democrats. One district in particular caused quite a stir: the 5th district with an African American majority, represented by Democrat representative Al Lawson. This district found itself split up into four others, each with a Republican majority. This came as a surprise to the entire Florida legislature, as the Fair Districts Act was very clear. Many believed that the new electoral map would be challenged in court and rejected by the Florida Supreme Court as it violates provisions of the Florida Constitution.

But the Florida Supreme Court, in June 2022, refused to rule on the issue, arguing that it did not fall within its jurisdiction. In doing so, it sent a strong message: the Florida Supreme Court refused to oppose Governor DeSantis. This allowed DeSantis to freeze his proposed electoral map until the November 2022 elections and to use it the way he wanted it, giving him a very strong Republican majority in the Senate and the House of Representatives.[3]

The legal battle is not over; it continues to unfold before the federal appeals court. If the case is brought one day before the nine sages of the federal Supreme Court, DeSantis the law scholar has already sharpened his arguments: he argues that the Fair Districts Act is itself unconstitutional because it is based on racial discrimination that runs counter to the principles of equality. But whatever the outcome of this legal battle, it would come long after the November 2022 elections, that Floridian Republicans won with a landslide.

Another tool DeSantis used was trying to control some voters' access to the ballot. Like many Republicans, DeSantis supports the loss of the right to vote for ex-convicts, and this category of voters are known to vote Democrat. In July 2022, DeSantis created the Office of Election Crimes and Security. Funded to the tune of three million dollars and made up of a 25-strong team, the aim of this Office is to investigate the allegedly immense electoral fraud in Florida.

In August 2022, some twenty people were arrested on suspicion of having voted in the previous 2020 elections when they were not entitled to do so.[4] Technically this was correct: DeSantis used a confusion in Florida law. In 2018, an amendment restored the right to vote to all ex-convicts who had

---

3 Gary Fineout, Florida Supreme Court Locks in DeSantis-Backed Redistricting Map, *Politico*, June 2, 2022.
4 Steve Contorno, Florida Police Cameras Show Police Arrests for Alleged Voter Fraud, *CNN*, October 19, 2022.

previously lost it, except for a small group of convicted murderers and sex offenders—the twenty or so people who were arrested. However, these people were encouraged by administrative staff to claim and regain their right to vote. They applied to be re-registered on the electoral roll, and this was approved, by mistake. These rehabilitated criminals thus received an electoral card and voted in 2020. However, despite the arrests by the police, prosecutors refused to prosecute them, saying they were all acting in good faith. Clearly, there was no malicious intent to fraud, and the case ended there. It does not appear that the Office of Election Crimes and Security uncovered any other fraudsters since that time. Ron DeSantis hasn't gained much from this story, apart from an effective publicity stunt that lent him an image of incorruptibility.

Governors in the United States do not usually get involved in local affairs at the county and city levels, but that is exactly what DeSantis did. He got personally involved in local elections, such as school districts, where a number of board positions are up for election every two years. There are 82 school districts in Florida, covering some 4,300 schools and 2.8 million students. DeSantis and some conservative PACs (Political Action Committee) publicly and financially supported highly politicized candidates in the school districts elections of November 2022, and this was unprecedented in the United States. School districts and boards of education had never been in the past a political battleground. In this respect, the strategy was innovative and unique, and the stakes were clear: this was an effort to control children's education. DeSantis could count on powerful PACs such as the "1776 PAC," which supported 49 candidates in Florida across 21 counties. Similarly, "Moms for Liberty," an association of conservative moms, was backing 12 Republican candidates. The Democrats entered the race late and only managed to back 20 candidates. In November 2022, 24 of the 30 candidates directly supported by DeSantis won their school districts elections.

In February 2023, DeSantis published a list of 14 school board members throughout Florida who were said to be "leftists" who had to be defeated, becoming a priority target of Republican candidates in the November 2024 elections.[5]

For universities, the strategy was more straightforward in that, under the Florida Constitution, the governor has the right to appoint 6 of the 13 members of the Board of Trustees of each public university. He can do so when a seat becomes vacant or when a member's term expires after five years. The entire

---

5   Amber Jo Cooper, DeSantis lays out 2024 Florida school board target list, *Florida's Voice*, February 22, 2023.

faculty and the president of the student council are each entitled to one member. The remaining five members are appointed by the Board of Governors,[6] who works closely with the governor.

The example of New College University reported by CNN[7] reflects this aspect of the DeSantis's strategy for education. New College is a liberal arts public university based in Sarasota, FL. It has just 700 students and was known until recently for its diversity and inclusion. Enrollment and graduation rates have been declining in recent years, and tuition fees are very high. New College was attracting interest from Republicans, who were wondering what was going on there with Florida taxpayers' money. It is a fair question; however, the very small number of students compared to the number of students at the University of Central Florida (approx. 60,000 students) or Florida Atlantic University (approx. 30,000 students) makes it difficult to understand why New College quickly became such a center of attention. In January 2023, DeSantis had the opportunity to appoint six trustees, which he did. However, it was rare for a governor to get so involved in university management. The following month, the president of New College was ousted by the now conservative Board of Trustees and replaced by a close DeSantis ally, Richard Corcoran, whose annual salary was set at $700,000, more than double that of his predecessor and certainly very high for such a small university.

Richard Corcoran[8] is an interesting character. He was Senator Marco Rubio's Chief of Staff and then Speaker of the Florida House of Representatives in 2016. Initially very critical of DeSantis, he became a close associate. DeSantis appointed him Florida's Education commissioner in 2021. Corcoran is against what he calls "woke indoctrination." At an event[9] at Hillsdale College, a private conservative school in Michigan, he proudly declared that he had a teacher fired for having a "Black Lives Matter" flag in her classroom.

For universities and schools alike, the stakes were clear as DeSantis himself said during his second inauguration speech in January 2023: "We must ensure

---

6 The Florida Board of Governors is a 17-member governing board that serves as the governing body for the State University System of Florida, which includes all public universities in the state of Florida.

7 Niquel Terry Ellis, Gov. DeSantis' Conservative Takeover of a Liberal Arts College Could Silence Diversity, Critics Say, *CNN*, February 17, 2023.

8 C.A. Bridges, Who is Richard Corcoran, the New Interim President of New College?, *Sarasota Herald Tribune*, February 14, 2023.

9 Ibid.

that our institutions of higher learning are focused on academic excellence and the pursuit of truth, not the imposition of trendy ideology."[10]

Another interesting cog in the DeSantis machine is the Florida Board of Medicine. Again, it is quite unusual for a governor to get involved in the appointment of members of the Board of Medicine. And yet here again, DeSantis would politicize this administration by supporting conservative doctors. It was his prerogative, and so he did it. He appointed many members to various boards, some of them financial donors to his election campaigns.[11]

This move allowed DeSantis to advance his own conservative agenda pertaining to transgender public policy. "The Florida Board of Medicine has a 12-member board of physicians who are technically independent of the state but are appointed by the governor and confirmed by the state Senate. By having Ladapo ask the Florida Board of Medicine to take executive action [on a complete ban on gender-affirming care for transgender minors], *DeSantis' administration essentially bypassed the Legislature and sped the process of enacting a ban on transition-related care*," says journalist Marc Caputo of NBC News.[12] At the end of 2022, the new Board of Medicine voted to prohibit any Floridian doctor from prescribing conversion therapies to transgender minors under 18, such as puberty blockers or hormone therapies; and from performing gender-change surgeries such as removal of breasts and genitals, which in any case are extremely rare for minors. Prior to this, the Board had already canceled reimbursement for medical therapies of transgenders. These therapies had previously been reimbursed under Medicare provisions.

DeSantis's tactics are efficient and permeate every level of civil society. Rarely has there been a governor so involved in every aspect of citizens' intimate, daily lives. With the support of the legislative bodies and the Florida Supreme Court, he showed his determination to redirect Florida's society toward a very conservative lifestyle. What is DeSantis' doctrine?

---

10 Zac Anderson, DeSantis Seeks to Transform Sarasota's New College with Conservative Board Takeover, *Herald Tribune*, January 9, 2023.

11 Sam Ogozalek, Florida Medical Board is Full of DeSantis Donors. They Vote on Transgender Care Friday, *Tampa Bay Times*, November 3, 2022.

12 Marc Caputo, DeSantis Moves to Ban Transition Care for Transgender Youths, Medicaid Recipients, *NBC News*, June 2, 2022.

PART 3

The DeSantis' Doctrine

CHAPTER 15

THE REPUBLICAN SOFTWARE

DeSantis is profoundly Republican, and all the main features of the Republican political matrix can be found in his doctrine today. He advocates a free economy and a minimum of federal intervention in the affairs of each state. In fact, he does not shy away from interventionism himself in Florida, but his position is rather: less government, but more efficiency.

Even so, he is not immune to a contradiction or two: DeSantis wants less federal government when it comes to taxes, but welcomes federal subsidies when Florida needs them. As he said it, in 2019 he managed to secure exceptional federal funding from Donald Trump to cover the cost of rebuilding part of Florida devastated by Hurricane Michael the previous year. Similarly, the state of Florida agreed to receive grants from Washington to revive the economy after the Covid-19-related recession, as well as to secure Covid-related medical equipment. Furthermore, in October 2022, following Hurricane Ian which struck the West Coast of Florida, killing 125 people and causing considerable damage, DeSantis received economic aid from Washington's emergency fund. For the occasion, Joe Biden and his wife traveled to the hard-hit town of Fort Myers to survey the damage, console communities, and to announce the $4 billion in federal aid to the state.

Regarding guns, DeSantis toes a purely Republican line. He favors the gun lobby, the powerful National Rifle Association (NRA), which gives him an A+ rating. Despite the national scourge of mass killings that also hit Florida in 2018 at Parkland High School, DeSantis is not interested in gun control. In 2022, he criticized the Florida Democrats for introducing a bill. Instead, he pledged to pass a law that would make it possible to carry a gun in Florida without a permit—which he did as of July 1, 2023—a position he has always supported.

Also unsurprisingly, like any Republican, DeSantis is profoundly anti-Communist. In May 2022, he signed a law declaring November 7th "Day for the Victims of Communism." On this day, teachers must teach high school students for at least 45 minutes about the dangers and crimes perpetrated by Communist regimes around the world. In schools and public offices, the day must be observed, but it is not a public holiday. To justify this law, DeSantis stated:[1] "At a time when marxism, socialism, and communism are actively promoted by prominent politicians and pop-culture figures in our own country, it is more important than ever to teach Florida's schoolchildren about the horrific history of Communist countries and to provide them with opportunities to hear from individuals who suffered under the rule of Communist dictators."

As is often the case with DeSantis, there are both personal and electoral reasons for this legislation. He is sincere in his fight against the violence of communist regimes, and in particular that of Cuba, which he knows well as the Cuban community is large and influential in Florida and his vice-governor Jeanette Núñez is originally from Cuba. Teaching children about the pitfalls of communism is important, but his opponents suggest that he should organize other similar days to pay tribute to the victims of other mass crimes, such as the massacre of Native American populations or the evils of slavery.

His anti-communist approach also has an electoral objective: Cuba is still under the yoke of a communist dictatorship today, and Florida has a vibrant Cuban community. In introducing the bill, DeSantis also mentioned Venezuela's political regime, which is extremely harsh on the population, but not communist per se. However, the Venezuelan population is growing rapidly in Florida. In fact, DeSantis attacked all forms of leftist dictatorship. He appealed to all Latin American minorities who have fled their countries and communist or non-communist dictatorships to live the American dream in the *Free State of Florida*, as he calls it. The Hispanic vote is strategic in Florida as it swings between Democrats and Republicans.[2] The Hispanic vote is a hotly contested one. In 2021, Florida's 22 million population was 27 percent Hispanic/Latino,[3] the majority of whom are Cubanos. By comparison, African Americans represent only 17 percent of the Floridian population and traditionally vote Democrat. DeSantis's strategy targeting the Hispanic vote

---

1 Ron DeSantis, Governor Ron DeSantis Declares First Annual Victims of Communism Day, www.flgov.com, November 7, 2022.

2 Laure Pallez and Nathalie Ponak, La Floride: un passage obligé pour Donald Trump!, *Personal Blog*, November 16, 2020.

3 U.S. Census Bureau, Quickfacts Florida.

has paid off, as was clear in the November 2022 midterms, when Florida's Latinos chose to vote massively (58 percent) in DeSantis's favor.[4]

Another element of the Republican matrix in recent years has been an unwavering support for law enforcement agencies. Along these lines, DeSantis invited leaders of law enforcement to the governor's personal mansion and strengthened their financial resources. To counter the impact of the *Defund the Police* movement, which followed in the wake of the murder of George Floyd in 2020, he passed a law prohibiting Florida municipalities and counties from cutting law enforcement budgets.

He also tried to pass a riot control law that he proudly called the toughest in the country.[5] In fact, there were relatively few *Black Lives Matter* riots in Florida, and they were less violent than in Chicago or New York. Yet this law is extremely tough: it prohibits blocking cars from circulating on a public street. But usually, demonstrations happen on the public streets. Also, drivers will not be prosecuted civilly if they cause injury or cause an accident involving protesters, if they can demonstrate that they were acting in self-defense. They could still face criminal penalties, but the law remains a scary prospect for ordinary peaceful demonstrators. It is sometimes difficult to extricate oneself from a demonstration which turns into a riot. Other elements of this law: a city council or any other local authority can no longer block the law enforcement sent by the governor to restore order in their town; arrested rioters will no longer be automatically released but will be brought before a court of justice; finally, destroying a plaque, statue, memorial, or flag becomes a second-degree offense.

Until June 2023,[6] this law, written in 2020 in the wake of the *Black Lives Matter* events, voted on and signed into law in April 2021, was subsequently deemed unconstitutional by a federal judge.

DeSantis, like all Florida governors before him and with genuine commitment, is doing much to preserve the Everglades National Park, which is threatened by severe pollution: toxic products, red algae blooms, and drying out threaten the entire ecosystem, which is a source of tourism revenue for the state. For 30 years, funding for Everglades preservation has come equally

---

4 Carmen Sesin, Why Florida Latinos turned out in favor of Republicans, *NBC News*, November 15, 2022.

5 Lalee Ibssa, What to Know About Florida's Anti-riot Law and the Corresponding Legal Challenge, *ABC News*, August 7, 2021.

6 Based on data as of June 2023.

from federal and state funding. In January 2022, the Biden administration's bipartisan Infrastructure Investment and Jobs Act promised an extraordinary $1.1 billion for Everglades restoration. This enabled the construction of a reservoir that will supply water to the whole of Florida Bay and the Everglades, preventing them from drying up too fast. The Everglades will continue their role as a carbon dioxide trap, and this federally funded work will protect access to drinking water for Floridians.

Recall that DeSantis alienated the Floridian sugar lobby when he was a representative in Washington. He refused to vote in favor of increased subsidies for Floridian sugarcane growers. Floridian sugarcane producers account for more than half of United States' total sugar production. Since the 1930s, an interventionist mechanism, never called into question by any party, has been put in place to limit sugar imports from other countries—they must represent a maximum of 15 percent of the total American market—and has established minimum prices set by the federal government. However, sugarcane generates large quantities of black smoke and requires large volumes of water. The Floridian sugar lobby is one of Florida's biggest polluters and benefits from historic agreements to pump the drinking water needed for its harvests from Lake Okeechobee, which further drains the lake and the Everglades.

In June 2022, going against decades of pro-sugar industry public policy, DeSantis vetoed a proposed law that would have given sugarcane growers even greater rights to Everglades water. In so doing, he sent a signal of independence from big industry. It was a surprising stance for a Republican, but really a blueprint for DeSantis's signature blend of pragmatism and interventionism. That said, it should be remembered that in April 2021, Governor DeSantis signed into law a de facto immunity for sugarcane farmers against lawsuits brought against them for pollution caused by the heavy black smoke.[7] Only residents living within 800 meters of sugarcane fields can lodge a complaint. This law constitutes a tremendous political concession to the sugar lobby.

While DeSantis is concerned about protecting the Everglades, he is more discreet about global warming. Yet Florida is directly threatened by global warming, as it is a state with very little topical relief and coastlines on both the Atlantic Ocean and the Gulf of Mexico, with vulnerability to hurricanes.[8]

---

7 Mary Ellen Klas, Florida Lawmakers Pass Bill to Shield Sugar Farmers from Lawsuits, *Tampa Bay Times*, April 22, 2021.
8 Laure Pallez, Rencontre avec David Michel, élu franco-américain du Connecticut, *Personal Blog*, June 2020.

According to a study by the Yale University Research Institute,[9] 73 percent of Floridians believe that global warming exists, and 70 percent believe that it will harm future generations. Moreover, 78 percent of Floridians also believe that the dangers of global warming should be taught in schools. Despite some Republicans' attempt to politicize the issue, most Floridians are very sensitive to and concerned about global warming. Ron DeSantis is aware of this, which surely explains why he is treading with caution on the subject. The Republican voters who make up the core of his electorate are rather distrustful of the scientific community.

In fact, DeSantis has an ambivalent relationship with science. His first instinct is to trust it—he himself has been vaccinated against Covid-19 and he was promoting the Covid vaccine during the first few months of its availability—but his respect for the scientific community's discourse grew relative. He questioned the effectiveness of masks and vaccines during the pandemic. He offered every American police officer a $5,000 bonus if they wished to move to Florida, including those officers dismissed for refusing to be vaccinated, making the state an eldorado for the unvaccinated.

At the same time, DeSantis-appointed Florida Surgeon General Joseph Ladapo advised against vaccinating healthy children, going against the recommendations of the CDC and the American Academy of Pediatrics. Ladapo also cited a study highly questioned by experts, which recommends that men aged 18 to 39 not be vaccinated.

In June 2022, DeSantis forced the organizing committee of the Special Olympics for individuals with intellectual disabilities to cancel the rule requiring all participants to be vaccinated against Covid-19. This population of athletes is particularly vulnerable in terms of health and care, and the organization protested, but DeSantis remained intractable. He threatened the committee with a $27 million fine if it kept the vaccination requirement for its athletes. The organizing committee eventually withdrew their request so as not to have to cancel the games.

Behind these bullying tactics, DeSantis's distrust of scientific doctrine may stem from a deep-seated skepticism, but it is also motivated by electoral opportunism. Today, it is hard to say where he stands on the crucial subject of global warming. What's more, his position may change in the future.

---

9 Climate Opinion Factsheets, Yale Program on Climate Change Communication, February 23, 2022.

CHAPTER 16

DESANTIS, EDUCATION, AND CRT

The term "woke" appeared in the United States in the African American community sporadically throughout the twentieth century. Martin Luther King wrote in his last book in 1968 before his death:[1] "Today, our very survival depends on our ability to stay awake, to adjust to new ideas, to remain vigilant and to face the challenge of change."

It wasn't until 2008 that the term gained notoriety, thanks to the RnB song *"Master Teacher,"* co-written by Erykah Badu and Georgia Anne Muldrow. In the chorus, the latter proclaims: "I stay woke." In a 2018 interview, she explained:[2] "Woke is definitely a black experience [...]. [It is] understanding what your ancestors went through. Just being in touch with the struggle that our people have gone through here and understanding we've been fighting since the very day we touched down here." Wokism is profoundly linked to slavery and the struggle of African Americans to achieve equal rights in the United States. It is therefore an African American concept that encourages us to be vigilant and to denounce acts of racism. The term did not spread significantly until 2013–2014, when it was seized upon by the *Black Lives Matter* movement. George Floyd's death in May 2020 gave the movement power, and the term "woke" entered the vernacular.

Today, wokism has expanded to offer a definition that would encompass all struggles against supposedly injustice to minorities: black minorities, of course, but also Asians and others; the fight against cultural appropriation; pro-LGBTQ+ rights; against religious discrimination. [...] To be white and to

---

1 Martin Luther King, Jr, Where Do We Go from Here: Chaos or Community, *Beacon Press*, 1968.
2 Elijah C. Watson, The Origin of Woke: How Erykah Badu And Georgia Anne Muldrow Sparked The "Stay Woke" Era, *Okay Player*, 2018.

claim to be woke is to recognize the inherent and fundamental nature of racism toward minority communities. In a way, this is like admitting that every white person is racist by default, and if they don't realize it, they are even more so.

What sets DeSantis apart from more traditional Republicans is his anti-progressive culture war against wokism. We have seen how the DeSantis machine works, and how, from 2020 to 2022, he was focused on education, from kindergarten to graduate school. His premise: public education is funded by citizens, so citizens have a say in what goes on in schools and universities. In the United States, a common core of education is recommended by Washington, but each state is responsible for the content of courses taught in public schools.

It is undeniable that faculties are predominantly politically leaning left across the country. A study by the Higher Education Research Institute at the University of California UCLA,[3] conducted among more than 20,000 professors across 143 public universities, estimates that over the period 2016–2017, 48 percent of faculty members considered themselves progressive; 12 percent far-left; 28 percent center or of no particular political color; 12 percent as conservative; 0.4 percent of faculty identified themselves as far-right. We know these proportions have changed very little over the years and are still valid in 2023. According to another study by the Pew Research Center[4] carried out in 2019, a majority of Americans expressed concern about the liberal politicization of universities and held suspicions about the admissions criteria and freedom of expression on the country's campuses.

In recent years, Republicans have attacked what they see as liberal indoctrination and launched numerous initiatives in universities. One example is the James Madison Constitutionalism Institute in Princeton, New Jersey. These institutes make a direct reference to the Founding Fathers, among whom James Madison is one of the most notable. Funded by private donors, they convey a traditional image of society and constitute an attempt by Republicans to rebalance political discourse on American campuses. Florida already has three similar institutes scattered across different campuses.

As a student at Yale University, DeSantis says he was shocked by the leftist and liberal proselytizing he observed there. He sees public universities as breeding grounds for Marxist political activism, teaching Critical Race

---

3 The HERI Faculty Survey, Undergraduate Teaching Faculty, 2016–2017.
4 The Growing Partisan Divide in Views of Higher Education, *The Pew Research Center*, August 19, 2019.

Theory (CRT), promoting Diversity, Equity, and Inclusion (DEI), and what he calls "gender ideology."

Before it came into the spotlight, CRT was the subject of a relatively little-known course in law schools to study the intersection between race, law, and the principle of equality. What does CRT, or Critical Race Theory, say? It states that race is a cultural concept invented to oppress people of color, and that American law and institutions are intrinsically racist. It calls into question certain popular ideas about racism, such as that it is the prerogative of a few bad people, or that some people are color-blind. CRT was developed in the 1970s by activists and researchers in the civil rights movement. It asserts that racism is systemic, that white privilege exists, and that the experience of the history and lives of people of color must be embraced and taught. According to Ron DeSantis, CRT creates all kinds of excesses in American schools:[5] some teach that all whites perpetuate systemic racism (schools in Buffalo, Portland), others celebrate black communism and the Black Panthers (a school in Philadelphia), others launch communication campaigns against whiteness in educational spaces (one of North Carolina's largest school districts).

In January 2023, at the same time as the offensive against the management of New College, DeSantis launched his major *Higher Education reform*, which touched on many subjects.[6] First and foremost, professors would have more control over what they teach, and as a result, would be less protected by the administration; they will be evaluated every five years instead of every ten years and can be fired if they fail to meet their objectives. Boards of directors and presidents would be able to request an evaluation of any teacher at any time. This reform gave administrators a right of review over the content of the courses offered to students.

Secondly, the reform offered more power to university boards of trustees over faculty recruitment, a power previously delegated to the faculty themselves. According to DeSantis, if a candidate for a teaching job today declares during a recruitment interview that he will treat all his students equally, whatever their skin color, he puts himself in a delicate position and loses points. DeSantis's perception (and what he disagrees with) is that a teacher is expected to give more support to people of color because he or she is expected to recognize the

---

5 Ron DeSantis, The Courage to Be Free: Florida's Blueprint for America's Revival, Broadside Editions, *Harper Collins Publications*, March 2023, pages 125–126.
6 Twitter @GovRonDeSantis, Governor DeSantis Announces Reforms for Florida's Higher Education, January 31, 2023.

theory of implicit bias, specifically racial bias, that is, to accept that by default all whites are biased and racist.

In his reform, DeSantis also announced the introduction of a core curriculum that would teach *"true"* history and philosophical values in Western society. But he maintained it is not about changing history. He asserted that America's history would be taught in its entirety, including the good and the bad, the tragedies and the triumphs, slavery, racial discrimination, and the civil rights movement.[7] In his eyes, it is more a question of not teaching students to hate their own country for the faults committed by their ancestors.

DeSantis also launched a new training course offered on an optional basis to Floridian teachers and schoolmasters, to reinforce civic education in schools and the teaching of the nation's founding principles, the U.S. Constitution, and key periods in American history from slavery to the Cold War. Those taking the course will receive a one-off bonus of $3,000. High school seniors will be given a civics test at the end of the academic year.

More controversially, DeSantis required all public universities to send the government a report detailing their spending on DEI programs, as well as their plans around CRT for the coming year, to estimate the cost associated with these programs. Then he announced the phasing out of the CRT, DEI,[8] and LGBTQ+ Rights Protection departments within public university administrative services.

Finally, he warned of the demise of any course inspired by or including the study of CRT, DEI, and "gender ideology" as he calls it. This includes Project 1619.[9] This project, based on a *New York Times* essay by Nikole Hannah-Jones published in 2019, proposes to put slavery and racism back at the center of U.S. history, arguing that the real date of the creation of the United States is not July 4, 1776, but rather the year 1619 when the first slaves arrived in then English colonies. The aim of the 1619 project is to open minds to critical thinking. Since the publication of this article, Project 1619 has been taught in several thousand American schools, but not in Florida. Governor DeSantis is

---

7 Ron DeSantis, The Courage to Be Free: Florida's Blueprint for America's Revival, Broadside Editions, *Harper Collins Publications*, March 2023, page 129.

8 According to Wikipedia, Diversity, equity, and inclusion refer to organizational frameworks that seek to promote the equitable treatment and full participation of all people.

9 Jake Silverstein, The 1619 Project and the Long Battle Over U.S. History, *The New York Times Magazine*, November 9, 2021.

strongly opposed to it, believing that certain elements of Project 1619 represent an erroneous rewriting of history. As he writes in his book, *"facts over narrative"*[10] must prevail and raw historical facts must take precedence over politicized narratives.

DeSantis's reform was a scandal. Andrew Gothard, president of the United Faculty of Florida, the Florida faculty union, declared:[11] "That's fundamentally anti-democratic. It's anti-American. Right. Every idea should have an opportunity to be discussed, debated, and explored on a higher education campus. And that right should not be abridged, simply because Governor DeSantis has decided that he doesn't like some ideas versus others." It's worth noting that DeSantis has previously launched an offensive against teachers' unions[12] demanding annual audits and tighter constraints on their activities on campuses and in schools.

"Education, not indoctrination" could be the summary of the essence of DeSantis message. For him, university must be a place of learning and education aimed at excellence, not politicization. The aim should be for students to seek the truth and learn to think for themselves. He believes that by training professors and administrative staff at CRT and DEI, public money is being spent unnecessarily, and that this helps to propagate left-wing political ideas.

As he presented his Reform for higher education, Ron DeSantis also highlighted the successes of his efforts over the past years, and they are significant. Tuition at Florida's public universities has not increased since 2018. Florida has the lowest tuition fees in the United States, and this is noteworthy especially in times of high economic inflation. It's also true that Florida's universities struggle to make it into the rankings of the best American universities. Gainesville is the best floridian university and ranks 44th[13] with 47,000 students.

Unusual for a Republican, DeSantis has made raising teacher salaries his hobbyhorse. Since 2018, more than a billion dollars has been invested in

---

10 Ron DeSantis, The Courage to Be Free: Florida's Blueprint for America's Revival, Broadside Editions, *Harper Collins Publications*, March 2023, page 129.

11 Amber Raub, Gov. DeSantis Asks State Public Universities to Report DEI and CRT Programs and Activities, *CBS12*, January 5, 2023.

12 Official page of Gov. Ron DeSantis, Governor Ron DeSantis Announces Unprecedented Legislation to Empower Educators, Protect Teachers from Overreaching School Unions and Raise Teacher Pay, January 23, 2023.

13 Topuniversities.com, The top 100 universities in USA.

raising salaries, increasing a young teacher's starting salary to $48,000 a year, and attracting more qualified profiles.

Another success story, this time in elementary and middle schools, is that the academic results of Florida's fourth graders and eighth graders have held up rather well against the Covid-19 pandemic, compared with the loss of momentum in other states.[14] Each year, the federal government tests these two school levels to define policies at the federal level. The latest national results are not good: student performance has dropped historically in math, and reading levels have fallen back to 1992 levels. In Florida, the math score fell by five points for fourth graders, which is substantial but in line with the national average; on the other hand, the reading level is stable compared with 2019. Middle schoolers fared less well, but Floridian fourth graders are ranked third in math and fourth in reading nationally.

This reinforced DeSantis and his convictions: his policy of keeping schools open during the pandemic worked. A glance at the results from California, which extended the school closure for a long time, shows that Californian students also performed rather well. Nothing conclusive one way or the other; nevertheless, it's a good result for Florida.

On the other hand, as of January 2023, the governor vetoed the content of the Advanced Program on African American studies, which is supposed to be taught in high school classes.[15] This course, which was offered to students for the first time in the fall of 2022, is aimed at the multidisciplinary study of the African American diaspora, covering literature, the arts, science, politics, and geography. It should be noted that these advanced courses are optional and chosen by students. There are many of them, on European history, art history, foreign languages and culture, and so on.

What the governor dislikes about the Advanced Program on African American studies is the inclusion in the curriculum of the study of the *Black Lives Matter* movement, black feminism and the black queer movement, as well as the study of the concept of "reparations," that is, to financially compensate for the harms of slavery. References to books that address the subjects of black communism and CRT are also critiqued. According to the Florida Department of Education, the course content contradicts the *Stop WOKE Act*

---

14 Nation's Report Card Shows Historic Drops in Math, Reading, *Orlando Sentinel*, October 24, 2022.

15 Nicole Chavez, Florida Officials Discussed AP African American Studies Course with College Board for Months before Initial Rejection, *CNN*, February 10, 2023.

signed in April 2022. According to this law, it is forbidden on Florida campuses to teach that everyone is inherently biased by race and held responsible for atrocities committed in the past by ancestors of the same skin color, gender, or nationality. To decipher, the goal is that children shouldn't feel guilty or anxious about crimes committed by their ancestors on Native Indian populations or on African Americans during slavery, nor should they feel ashamed of their country. DeSantis believes, for example, that it's wrong to say that the country was built on stolen territory.

While his positions resonate with a segment of the American population, his detractors accuse him of wanting to whitewash American history. According to them, American history is a painful story.

Faced with this reform, we can expect a form of self-censorship on the part of teachers. Parents now have the right to take them to court if they feel that a lesson has touched on topics of race or gender that are forbidden and/or make pupils uncomfortable. Teachers' unions report having received instructions from some school districts not to wear rainbow-colored clothing or have a photo of their same-sex spouse, or even to remove the *safe space* stickers from their office doors. Overall, we can expect less support and visibility for young students from racial and sexual minorities in Florida universities.

CHAPTER 17

DESANTIS AND THE RIGHTS OF THE LGBTQ+ COMMUNITY

In June 2021, DeSantis signed the Fairness in Women's Sports Act. This law requires athletes to compete on the team of the sex assigned to them at birth: girls and women on female teams, boys and men on male teams, even if they have transitioned to female in the meantime (or vice versa). In this, DeSantis is following a trend that already exists in over twenty-five states where similar laws are under discussion or have already been passed.

The following year, in March 2022, he signed into law the Individual Freedom Act, nicknamed Stop WOKE (Stop Wrong to Our Kids), banning the teaching of Critical Race Theory (CRT), which we discussed in the previous chapter. This law was followed the next month by The Parental Rights in Education Act, nicknamed Don't Say Gay by its opponents, a law limiting freedom of expression about gender identity and sexual orientation in Florida schools. These two laws are highly controversial and might be considered a brake on the freedom of expression not only of teachers but also of children in the context of their school.

What exactly does the Don't Say Gay law say? Parents have the "fundamental" right to choose how their children are educated and raised. This means that this right is not granted by the government to citizens but is fundamental and cannot be taken away by any government. As a result, parents are the ultimate authority for all decisions relating to their children's education. And so the law says, for example, that schools do not have the right to withhold any information about their children's mental, emotional, or physical health from parents.

Another element of the Don't Say Gay law is that teachers are forbidden from talking about sexual orientation or gender identity in elementary classes up to third grade. These are not subjects that teachers usually discuss in class with very young children. Yet groups such as Moms for Liberty[1] believe that there is a new, ultra-progressive generation of teachers who are encouraging conversations around gender transition in the classrooms, and that these conversations should be reserved for the family circle. Opponents of the law, on the contrary, believe that school should remain a safe space for children who can't or don't dare broach these subjects at home.

What bothers the law's advocates is that children themselves can discuss these subjects with their teachers without their families knowing. The Parental Rights in Education Act states that it is now forbidden for a teacher to hide from parents the fact that their child has chosen to change pronouns and given names. This kind of complex case has already occurred, for example in California, where a school principal asked a teacher to hide a student's gender transition from their parents, as required by California law. The teacher refused to do so because she felt it went against her religious principles.

A scenario discussed by opponents of the law is that of a child from a same-sex family. If the child draws his/her family, or simply mentions their two dads or two moms in class, or asks questions about his/her family structure, this can trigger a discussion between students and the teacher about homosexuality. Parents who feel embarrassed by this discussion can now file a complaint against the teacher. This raises the question of whether the children should censor themselves so as not to endanger their teacher or offend the sensibilities of their classmates.

DeSantis clarified his position in an interview in May 2023:[2] uttering the word "gay" at school is not forbidden, he said. When asked by the journalist whether a teacher has the right to say that he or she is gay—a subject that may come up in a discussion with his or her students—DeSantis replies that the law doesn't forbid it. But he wouldn't want a teacher to tell a child that he or she was "born in the wrong body," or for there to be any form of encouragement to change gender. According to him, 70 percent of parents surveyed in Florida support the law. He also pointed out that the teaching of sex education is not prohibited: it is the responsibility of each school district in Florida, as it is not mandatory at the state level. In practice, parents are informed in advance of these two half-day courses and can request, if they wish, that their children

1 Paige Williams, The Right-wing Mothers Fuelling the School Board Wars, *The New Yorker*, October 31, 2002.

2 Interview given to John Stossel, *You Tube*, May 2023.

not be taught and remain in the library until the human development course is over.

As for the Stop WOKE Act, the law prohibits talking about CRT, as we've seen. Under Corcoran, then Secretary of Education in 2021, the Department of Education had already attempted to ban CRT from K–8 classrooms. Here we must point out that CRT was never included in the academic curriculum of elementary and middle schools. Therefore, Corcoran's approach was purely theoretical. The Stop WOKE Act of 2022 is a form of extension of this attempt, pushing the ban to high schools, colleges, and universities. In November 2022, a federal judge in Florida blocked the law for colleges and universities, deeming it dystopian:[3] "If important questions about our democracy cannot be discussed in the classroom, democracy will sink into obscurantism." DeSantis's team has promised to appeal. Nevertheless, the Stop WOKE law and the interdiction to teach CRT is already being applied in schools across Florida.

As a result of these two laws, over 200 books were banned from Florida school libraries, most of them dealing with racial themes: Ibrahim Kendi's *How to Be an Antiracist*; Toni Morrison's *The Bluest Eye*. Other books deal with sexual themes: Judy Blume's *Forever*; Aldous Huxley's *Brave New World*, accused of being too overtly sexual, of using too vulgar language, and of glorifying drugs. Other books deal with gender identity: *Two Boys Kissing* by David Levithan; *Gender Queer: A Memoir* by Maia Kobabe. All the schools have reviewed the content of their shelves to ensure that they do not place themselves in a position of illegality.

In addition, DeSantis banned 41 percent of widely used math textbooks from Florida schools. Certain textbooks were banned because they were considered to promote CRT. For example, a book that said "United States has not eradicated poverty or racism" was banned because it was considered to emphasize that the United States was a poor or racist country, and had an element of CRT with political significance. According to its objectors, it could cause emotional distress to a young student who would be saddened to find that his or her country is poor or racist.

Other topics covered in rejected textbooks include math problem texts that focus on the wage difference between men and women, the declining white population in the United States, social justice, global warming, or vaccines. Finally, textbooks containing references to social behaviors and an emotional

---

3 Ben Brasch, Judge Nikes Higher Education Portions of Florida Stop WOKE Act, *The Washington Post*, November 18, 2022.

approach to learning (how to deal with math anxiety, for example) were also banned.[4]

There are many voices opposing these two laws, which is certain to drive teachers to self-censorship. One of these voices can be heard around the world, and it's that of the progressive Disney company. The company is known for developing cartoons that keep pace with the changing mores of the American population:[5] Snow White, Cinderella, and Sleeping Beauty have gradually been replaced by the rebellious Ariel (*The Little Mermaid*), Pocahontas and Mulan, and more recently by Elsa (*Frozen*), Moana and Merida, the heroine of *Brave*. The latter are strong characters who are in control of their lives and don't need male characters at their side. In *Strange World*, Disney's latest animated feature released in 2022, the main character's son Ethan is openly in love with his friend, a boy named Diazo. This is the first time an openly homosexual character has appeared in a popular cartoon.

In March 2022, a veritable cold war broke out between the governor and the powerful corporation, which is Florida's second largest employer (after Publix) with over 80,000 people in the Orlando area.[6] While the law does not directly concern the company or its operations, CEO Bob Chapek is an outspoken critic, driven by internal pressure from his employees and Walt Disney's granddaughter, herself a member of the LGBTQ+ community. The dispute quickly flared up. Ron DeSantis, who got married at Disney World Resort in 2009, famously said: "If Disney wants to pick a fight, they chose the wrong guy."

To prove his good faith to his employees, Chapek promised to donate five million dollars to LGBTQ+ rights organizations and announced the suspension of Disney's political donations—in other words, it will stop funding Republicans. Disney had given $125,000 to the Florida GOP in 2021, and $90,000 to support individual Republican candidates. Since the beginning of this feud, some Republican elected officials have returned part of these sums to Disney.

What levers does the governor have at his disposal to respond to Disney? Since 1967, Disney has enjoyed a special status in Florida: it's a kind of state

---

4 Moriah Balingit, DeSantis Accused Textbooks of "Indoctrination." Here's What he Meant, *The Washington Post*, May 9, 2022.

5 Richard Gray, Did Disney Shape How You See the World?, *BBC*, July 31, 2019.

6 Jesus Jimenez and Brooks Barnes, What We Know About the DeSantis-Disney rift, *New York Times*, February 27, 2023.

within a state, a kind of government that operates autonomously. Disney makes its own decisions on urban planning and has its own tax system, or rather, taxes itself, which enables it to finance its emergency medical and security services, and even part of its electricity. In this way, the company has saved significant amounts in taxes, even though the way it operates (road maintenance, buses, hotels) is costly.

On the other hand, it has also accumulated almost a billion dollars in debt, and if its special status were to disappear, it would be up to the citizens of the surrounding counties not only to repay the debt but also to assume Disney's operational costs. Floridian legislators—under the aegis of DeSantis—decided to rein in their ardor against the park's management and eventually allowed it to retain its special status.

But on February 27, 2023, a new law limiting Disney's prerogatives was endorsed by DeSantis, who declared:[7] "Disney came out against something that was really just about protecting young kids, and making sure that students are able to go to school learning to read, write, add, subtract, and not having a teacher tell them that they can change their gender. And I think most parents agree with that." He also added, "Today, the corporate kingdom finally comes to an end. There's a new sheriff in town, and accountability will be the order of the day. Buckle up."

Despite the conquering communication, Disney will still not be taxable in Florida.[8] The main change is that the county with special administrative status in which Disney is located will now be governed by a five-member Board of Directors appointed by DeSantis. This board will manage Disney's municipal services and infrastructure, with a say in the development of new attractions in the park. Previously, members of this board were personalities with ties to Disney. The five new members include Martin Garcia, a Republican activist lawyer who donated $50,000 to the DeSantis election campaign, and Bridget Ziegler, co-founder of the *Moms for Liberty* movement and wife of Christian Ziegler, the new chairman of the Republican Party of Florida.

Before concluding this chapter, it's important to point out that American society is overwhelmingly progressive considering gay marriage and women's rights. According to a 2019 Pew Research Institute poll,[9] 72 percent of the

---

7 Steve Contorno and Kit Maher, DeSantis Signs Bill that Gives Him More Control of Disney's Special District, *CNN*, February 27, 2023.

8 Ibid.

9 The Global Divide on Acceptance of Homosexuality, *Pew Research Center,* June 24, 2020.

population believe that homosexuality should be accepted by society, a figure corroborated by more recent polls.[10]

In 2015, the Supreme Court issued a landmark ruling allowing same-sex marriage in all states. Following the Court's June 2022 reversal on abortion, concerned Democrats then pushed to enshrine marriage for all in federal law. This was not the case for abortion rights, left with no protection other than the Supreme Court ruling. In November 2022, 12 of the 50 Republican senators joined the 50 Democrat senators to vote in favor of the law allowing marriage for all in all 50 U.S. states. In December 2022, the bill came back before the House of Representatives, where 39 Republican representatives joined the Democrats in approving it.

Signed into law by Joe Biden on December 13, 2022, the bipartisan legislation enshrines the right to marriage for all in federal law, guaranteeing that even in the event of a Supreme Court reversal, this right is now protected and intangible.

---

10 Homosexuality in the United States—Statistics and Facts, *Statista Research Department*, November 9, 2022.

CHAPTER 18

ABORTION AND RELIGION

Abortion is a profound moral issue that today pits pro-lifers versus pro-choicers in the United States and beyond. DeSantis is fundamentally pro-life and vows to fight to reduce access to abortion in Florida. This highlights one of the great paradoxes of the right he represents: advocating individual freedom for everyone but restricting it when it comes to women's bodies.

Republicans have not always been overwhelmingly anti-abortion.[1] In June 1967, Ronald Reagan, then governor of California and already a Republican, signed one of the most permissive laws in favor of abortion for Californians. As we know, in 1973, the famous U.S. Supreme Court case *Roe v. Wade* made the right to abortion constitutional. In the 1960s and early 1970s, those opposed to abortion were mainly evangelicals, who represented around 25 percent of the American population at the time and were either Democrats or Republicans. Overall, the voters' opinion on abortion rights was fairly balanced whatever the political color:[2] the subject remained in the realm of the private and religious sphere, and everyone took a position according to his or her own conscience.

What happened since? By electoral strategy, the evangelical current of thought was identified and recuperated by the Republicans. Spurred on by such vocal figures as American far-right strategist Paul Weyrich and anti-feminist lawyer Phyllis Schlafly, Republicans saw an opportunity: to recapture evangelical votes by promising to repeal the legislation on abortion. In 1980, Ronald Reagan, then a candidate for the U.S. presidential election, campaigned in an extraordinary about-face against abortion and won the evangelical votes. This was a major factor in his victory, and he was elected president. The strategy was a winning one and has since been adopted by

---

1 The History of Abortion Politics, *Institute for Policy Research*, August 16, 2022.
2 Abortion Trends by Party Identification, *Gallup*, 2022.

most Republican candidates. In 1999, long before he entered politics, Donald Trump declared in an interview on NBC: "I am very much pro-choice." In 2016, the same Donald Trump declared during a speech on the campaign trail: "The mother and the doctor decide together to kill a fetus? I don't think so!" He won 81 percent of the evangelical vote, helping him to become the 45th president of the United States.

Since that election, the national-conservatism movement (also known as *NatCon*) supported Trump and his successors. The *NatCons*, as they call themselves, are a movement of ideas that provide language and concepts for right-wing American politicians. As French researcher Maya Kandel aptly describes in a study for IFRI,[3] the influence of these conservative Catholic, Protestant, and Jewish intellectuals on the conservative wing and the policies of the Republican politicians is undeniable. They advocate a "non-liberal, Christian political system [...] that often invokes the model defined by Viktor Orban in Hungary."[4] Among his exploits, Hungary's ultra-conservative prime minister Viktor Orban signed a decree in September 2022 forcing pregnant women wishing to have an abortion to listen to the fetal heartbeat.

What we're seeing today since *Roe v. Wade* was overturned in June 2022 is that a majority of Americans is angry: polls show that most of them are in favor of some form of abortion access. Society has evolved since the 1970s. Besides, not all evangelicals are against abortion rights these days. The overturning of *Roe v. Wade* benefits indirectly the Democrats, who held up rather well in the November 2022 midterm elections. Some Republicans are even retreating on the subject, uncomfortable with having to implement restrictive laws in their states, laws that are certainly unpopular but which they had promised their constituents for years and which have now become reality.

In Florida, in July 2022, a new law lowered the legal time limit for abortion from 24 weeks to 15, and then to 6 weeks in July 2023, except under certain circumstances. By way of comparison, the legal time limit in France is 14 weeks. In fact, Florida had become something of an eldorado for abortion: the 24-week deadline—almost the end of the second trimester—was particularly permissive, and many women came from other states to have abortions in Florida as the laws were stricter in their own states. This is no longer the case.

---

3 Maya Kandal, Le national-conservatisme, quelle politique étrangère pour la "nouvelle droite" américaine ?, Institut Français des Relations Internationales, March 10, 2023.
4 Ibid.

Abortion is no longer permitted in cases of rape or incest. Abortion is only possible after the legal 15 weeks—and now 6 weeks—if there is a serious risk to the mother's health, or a lethal abnormality of the fetus. According to a report in *The Guardian*,[5] a Florida couple was refused an abortion in February 2023, even though their case could have been considered a special circumstance: their fetus (over 15 weeks old) suffered from very serious abnormalities, and if the pregnancy continued, the baby would have died before delivery or at best a few minutes afterward. In this tragic case, the doctors, advised by their lawyers, refused to sign the abortion authorization. Sadly, the new legislation is destabilizing and distressing the medical profession, which in that case was erring on the side of caution, to the detriment of both mother and child.

Tampa's prosecutor, Democrat Andrew Warren, declared in August 2022 that he would not use his office to go after people who seek and provide abortions or on doctors that provide gender affirming care to transgender people.[6] The democratically elected lawmaker was then suspended from office by Ron DeSantis in an unprecedented move, accusing Warren of neglect of duty and incompetence. Pushing back the limits of the governor's power, DeSantis justified his action by denouncing that no individual has the right to place themselves above the laws of Florida.

What drives DeSantis' anti-abortion flame is his faith, which comes from his mother. She comes from a particularly religious family. She has a brother who is a priest and a sister who is a nun. Moreover, DeSantis's public persona is rooted in religion. He conveys the values of the traditional Christian family. In July 2022, he filed a complaint over a Miami bar, threatening to take away its liquor license because the owners had organized a drag show and children were in the audience. According to DeSantis's press release, the event corrupted public morals and was indecent. He was widely applauded or criticized across the country for this decision, once again very divisive.

About religion, DeSantis multiplied the use of evangelical vocabulary during his 2022 election campaign. In February 2022, addressing students at the private conservative Hillsdale College in Michigan, DeSantis declared: "Put on the full armor of God. Stand firm against the left's schemes. You will face flaming arrows, but if you have the shield of faith, you will overcome them, and in Florida we walk the line here. And I can tell you this, I have only begun

---

5 Maya Yang, Florida Couple Unable to Get Abortion, *The Guardian*, February 18, 2023.
6 Steve Contorno, DeSantis Suspends Tampa Prosecutor Who Took Stance Against Criminalizing Abortion Providers, *CNN*, August 4, 2022.

to fight."[7] As we know, the rhetoric of violence must be used sparingly, as there is a great risk of stirring up hatred and encouraging extremist groups to act, as we saw with the attack on the Capitol on January 6, 2021. Yet DeSantis uses elements of combative Christian rhetoric throughout his campaign, flirting with Christian nationalist circles.

In an interview for the Christian podcast Focus on the Family in June 2022,[8] he declared:

"They are trying to establish a religion of their own, this woke ideology functions as a religion. Obviously, it's not the Judeo-Christian tradition, but they want that to be, effectively, the governing faith of our country. They want that to be the core orthodoxy in public schools and in other types of public functions. And so, they want to impose their values."

While he is not the only politician to use religious dialectics, he is one of the first to compare wokism to a religion.

On November 4, 2022, four days before the election for his re-election as governor of Florida, his wife Casey posted on her Twitter account a campaign ad[9] filmed in black and white, in which a deep voice introduced Ron DeSantis as God's protector and fighter, said to have created him on day 8. The phrase *"God made a fighter"* is repeated five times during the spot, which lasts less than two minutes. DeSantis's mission is no small feat: he must save people's jobs, their livelihoods, their liberty, and their happiness. The short video deliberately leaves room for doubt at the end: at no point is it made clear whether Ron DeSantis is to save the people of Florida or the people of the United States.

---

7 Ana Ceballos, What Message is DeSantis sending with "Full Armor of God" Rhetoric?, *Tampa Bay Times*, September 12, 2022.

8 Ron DeSantis interview, Being a Positive Force for the Family, *Focus on the Family Podcast*, June 23, 2022.

9 Twitter @CaseyDeSantis, November 4, 2022.

CHAPTER 19

IMMIGRATION

Immigration to the United States has created a "Nation of Nations," as President John F. Kennedy put it. Yet the question that remained at the heart of U.S. immigration policies for decades is which modes of regulation to use. In France, the immigration bill painfully voted in 2023 by the Parliament attempts to, on the one hand, facilitate the regularization of undocumented workers and, on the other, facilitate their deportation. This clearly illustrates the paradox that France—and the United States—are facing: the need for foreign labor in jobs in short supply is in conflict with the desire for immigration control expressed by citizens at the ballot box.[1]

In the United States, Joe Biden announced that he wants to tighten up the rules for welcoming illegal immigrants at the border at a time when America is suffering from a labor shortage to carry out its major infrastructure projects. It is estimated that over two million illegal immigrants arrived in the United States in 2022 alone.[2] This is a record number. The migrants come mainly from Venezuela, Cuba, and Nicaragua. The three main receiving states are California (24 percent), Texas (11 percent), and Florida (10 percent). The "open border" with Mexico, as DeSantis calls it, has also been blamed for the opioid crisis. Drugs, and fentanyl in particular, enter the U.S. territory easily.

According to research done in 2020 by the Pew Research Institute,[3] the United States has more immigrants than any other country in the world. More than forty million people living in the United States were born in another

---

1 Flore Kayl and Laure Pallez, L'immigration aux États-Unis, au-delà du clivage gauche-droite, *Fondation Jean Jaurès*, April 19, 2023.
2 Julia Ainsley, Migrant Border Crossings in Fiscal Year 2022, *NBC News*, October 22, 2022.
3 Abby Budiman, Key Findings about U.S. Immigrants, *Pew Research Institute*, August 20, 2020.

country, representing 12 percent of the country's 332 million inhabitants and a fifth of the world's migrants. In addition to legal immigrants, the United States has an estimated eleven million illegal immigrants.

In France, the regularization of illegal immigrants has traditionally been a left-wing claim, and tighter borders a right-wing position. But in the United States, the lines are more flexible: Republicans have historically supported business-oriented immigration, that is, immigration that provides the skilled but also unskilled foreign labor needed for big American companies to prosper. Democrats usually support more humane immigration, open to political refugees and asylum seekers.

At every Democrat convention, the candidates declare that they are in favor of funding healthcare expenses for irregular migrants. Paradoxically, these positions are in line with the agenda of the American Republican business community, which favors cheaper labor from Central and South America, especially as it means putting downward pressure on American wages.

In 2013, the bipartisan Gang of Eight bill came close to passing in Congress, aiming at both simplifying the regularization of the then eleven million illegal migrants and tightening border controls. Left-right lines were blurred about immigration, and alliances sometimes improbable. However, in 2013, despite a Republican-majority House of Representatives, the bipartisan bill failed because a group of ultra-right-wing deputies opposed any mass regularization on principle. Ron DeSantis was one of them. It was perhaps this 2013 movement that would later inspire Donald Trump: in 2016 when he campaigned on building a wall along the Mexican border, he opposed traditional business-oriented Republicans.

Border control is the responsibility of the federal government. In 2023, forced to act, the Biden administration was considering control measures, while keeping in mind the need for manpower and the regularization of illegal immigrants. Ron DeSantis faced the same dilemma in Florida: his state needs a low-skilled workforce to support its economic growth. At the same time, DeSantis has made the fight against illegal immigration his own. He followed in Donald Trump's footsteps, regularly denouncing the hypocrisy of the Republican leadership in Washington and its disconnection from the electoral base.

A governor's leeway to control immigration in his state is slim. In 2019, DeSantis proclaimed the cancellation of sanctuary city status for 28 Florida municipalities. Until then, these cities or counties enjoyed a status that allowed them to protect undocumented migrants. Local police were not obliged to report them to federal authorities. Since 2019, in these 28 municipalities as in the rest of the state, police officers must cooperate with federal authorities and set up identification procedures for all undocumented migrants.

In September 2022, DeSantis organized—with the money of fellow Floridian citizens—the airlifting of migrants between Texas and the exclusive pro-Democrat Massachusetts island of Martha's Vineyard. Beyond the questionable and not new practice (Texas governor was frequently doing the same), DeSantis's message was clear: it is easy to lecture states like Florida, Texas, and California and theorize about regularizing undocumented immigrants from Washington or Massachusetts. But welcoming them physically and integrating them into civil society is far more complex on the ground. With this dubious stunt, he was forcing the Democrats to face up to the problem of immigration.

PART 4

The New Strongman of the Republican Right

CHAPTER 20

REPUBLICAN TROUBLES

In 2022, DeSantis campaigned for re-election as governor of Florida, and emerged victorious. His slogan was "Keep Florida Free," a direct allusion to his libertarian policies during the Covid-19 pandemic. Victory was easy, not only because of the mechanics of the campaign, but also because of his opponent's weakness. Charlie Crist is a politician of the previous generation, more at ease in large campaign rallies than on television. During the TV debate between the two men, broadcast just before the election, Charlie Crist addressed the small troop of supporters who came to support him in the TV studio, while Ron DeSantis stared directly into the camera. Two generations of politicians clashed, as did two visions of the world.

So DeSantis won re-election by a landslide, a shock in the post-midterm election political landscape in November 2022. His insolent victory presented a profound contrast with the weak performance at the national level of the Republican Party: despite the "red wave" that had been expected, the Republicans failed to regain control of the Senate, which remained under a Democrat majority (51 votes to 49). They also performed poorly in the House of Representatives, where they nonetheless won a majority with 222 seats to 213 for the Democrats. They needed 218 to gain control, so their majority was very narrow.

Frustration among Republicans, pointing the finger at each other to identify the culprits behind this low score, led to one name on everyone's lips: Donald Trump. The candidates he has supported have not fared well. Whereas in the past, Trump's support was a guarantee of victory for the candidates, it seemed that he lost his power of influence and was no longer the kingmaker.

What's more, it was no longer enough to be financed and parachuted in by a major party or backed by the boss to win; you also must be a legitimate candidate, rooted in the local fabric. The case of Trump-backed Dr. Mehmet Oz is telling: the surgeon is a TV celebrity. Parachuted in by the Republican

Party in Pennsylvania to run for the Senate in Washington, he lost out to John Fetterman, the ailing Democrat candidate. Another example: the Republican candidate for Georgia senator Herschel Walker, endorsed by Donald Trump. During his campaign, the former NFL player, who campaigned against abortion rights, was accused by an ex-girlfriend of having given her money to pay for her abortion. Herschel Walker's son added: his father extolled traditional moral values, but he is said to have fathered four children from unions with four different women, none of whom he raised or lived with. When his ex-wife claimed that he threatened her with a pistol at point-blank range, the Republican candidate claimed not to remember the episode, as he suffered from dissociative personality disorder—which he has been treated for ever since. His shaky candidacy cost him victory, but surprisingly by a narrow margin: he lost by just 40,000 votes, with 48.5 percent of the vote to his Democrat opponent Raphael Warnock's 49.4 percent. But above all, his defeat weakened Trump.

Another lesson from this election was that the deniers who still refuse to acknowledge the results of the 2020 election, supported by Donald Trump, have largely lost their elections. While DeSantis used some of his campaign funds to support some of these deniers in Florida, he has cautiously never officially corroborated Trump's narrative in relation to the supposedly rigged and stolen elections. The deniers' defeats weakened Donald Trump even further. In November 2022, Republicans were beginning to doubt the ex-president's ability to win not just the presidential election in 2024, but all the other elections taking place at the same time, in the House of Representatives, the Senate, and all the local elections.

As for the democratic process, the elections went rather smoothly and calmly: fears of reliving the violent scenes of the 2020 presidential elections were on the minds of polling station volunteers. In the end, these elections show that Americans want a return to respect for institutions and democracy, with candidates of higher quality and greater integrity.

Since those elections, the GOP has been in turmoil. The painful election of Kevin McCarthy as Speaker of the House revealed the different factions and the growing weight of the Freedom Caucus. The Republican Party is divided, with several more or less vocal factions rubbing shoulders and sometimes avoiding each other.

As proof, at the annual Conservative Political Action Conference (CPAC) on March 4, 2023, Donald Trump occupied the podium for two hours, while other major Republican political figures were conspicuous by their absence. Ron DeSantis, Mike Pence, and many governors who once considered CPAC a must-attend event did not make the trip in 2023. The convention has lost its luster. A decade ago, it drew 10,000 people; in 2023, they were less than 2,200. Moreover, journalists from Fox News did not attend, something that would have been unthinkable just a few years ago. The CPAC convention is no longer really the gathering place for all conservatives, and many interest groups, such as the highly influential 500,000-member Heritage Foundation,[1] did not attend. Likewise, the wealthy Club for Growth,[2] with over 500,000 anti-tax, pro-free enterprise members, was a no-show.

Sign of further division, the Club for Growth was organizing a retreat on the same dates as CPAC at the Breakers Hotel in Palm Beach—three miles from Donald Trump's Mar-a-Lago residence—featuring Ron DeSantis, Mike Pence, Mike Pompeo, Trump's former secretary of state, Virginia governor Glenn Youngkin, and former South Carolina governor Nikki Haley. The ultimate affront: Donald Trump was not invited.

Despite this turmoil, in May 2023, at a time when public institutions were feared to be at a standstill with the potential shutdown of public services, Republican Speaker Kevin McCarthy managed to negotiate an increase in the U.S. public debt ceiling, just before the June 1st deadline.[3] He had to navigate between Democrat spending and Freedom Caucus budgetary rigor. He obtained from the Democrats a temporary freeze on spending in numerous sectors (education, transportation, healthcare, veterans' subsidies, law enforcement, etc.) and the repatriation to Washington of unused post-Covid aid. At the same time, he confirmed a bipartisan agreement to increase the U.S. defense budget by +3 percent and to set up a special force of U.S. tax agents to hunt down tax evaders among the wealthiest citizens.

---

1 Website: https://www.heritage.org/.

2 Website: https://www.clubforgrowth.org/.

3 Jarrett Renshaw, What's in the Debt Ceiling Deal Struck by Biden and McCarthy?, *Reuters*, May 28, 2023.

CHAPTER 21

THE TRUMP–DESANTIS RIVALRY

A week after the November 8, 2022, election, Donald Trump announced his candidacy for the next presidential election in 2024. Politically weakened, he was still physically fit and strongly supported by the Republican base. By running so early, two years before the election, he hoped to mark his territory on the right and scare off the other Republican candidates. What Donald Trump is seeking by running may be to dodge his serious legal problems in the hope of regaining presidential immunity, but it's more likely that it's his inflated ego that is driving him.

But from now on, Republicans doubt his ability to win the presidency. More than anything, what Republicans want in 2024 is a Republican president, whoever it may be. The question is: Who has the best chance of winning against a Democrat candidate? Back in spring 2023, polls did not show Donald Trump as a possible winner versus Biden. Tables turn fast in politics.

Apart from Ron DeSantis, other names were being mooted among Republicans. Since the attack on the Capitol on January 6, 2021, by American ultra-right extremists fired up by Donald Trump's diatribes, Mike Pence has accused Trump of endangering his family and the lives of everyone who worked on Capitol Hill. Some of the demonstrators chanted "Hang Mike Pence" as he was already perceived as a traitor then since he didn't oppose the November 2020 election results virulently enough. His candidacy would have a hard time rallying people around him, and his evangelical base is pretty thin. While he is more respectful in temperament than Trump, he did claim credit for the results of the Pence–Trump administration and supported the ban on abortion and same-sex marriage.

Other possible candidate: Nikki Haley, Ambassador to the United Nations and former governor of South Carolina. But in November 2022, Ron DeSantis's name was on everyone's lips. Like Trump, both live in Florida, and both see themselves as outsiders to the establishment. But the comparisons end there. They come from different social backgrounds: Donald Trump comes from New York high society, while Ron DeSantis comes from Florida middle-class. Donald Trump is impetuous and moody, DeSantis is competent and poised. Their academic backgrounds are the opposite of each other: according to his niece Mary Trump,[1] young Donald is a brawling, bullying heir, whom his father sends to a New York military academy at the age of 13 to straighten him out. In contrast, DeSantis was an academic and sporting star throughout his school career. Trump came late to politics, whereas DeSantis started at the age of 32.

In his biography,[2] Ron DeSantis explains why virtually the entire Republican Party opposed Trump in 2016. He relates that Donald Trump has in the past financially supported Democrat personalities such as a certain Hillary Clinton, and that he was in favor of pro-abortion laws and restricting gun rights. Finally, DeSantis reminded the reader that Trump did everything in his power to avoid military service. These reminders are not innocent: they serve to highlight DeSantis's own determination, the fact that he has never deviated from his conservative values, and his military experience as a decorated officer on numerous occasions.

The Republican base that supports Donald Trump is extremely loyal to him. In 2016, it represented 45 percent of Republican voters, but by spring 2023 polls gave him around 60 percent of favorable votes. The greater the number of candidates, the more difficult it will be for one candidate to rally as many supporters as Donald Trump. So he has every chance of once again becoming the Republican Party's nominee, unless all the other candidates rally behind a single candidacy.

Trump understood this and encouraged as many candidates as possible. He also surrounded himself with his loyal ally, lobbyist, and campaign manager Susie Wiles. We know she worked on Ron DeSantis's gubernatorial campaign in 2018 and was abruptly fired by him. So this move by Trump is clever, as Susie Wiles knows the inner workings of the DeSantis machinery and will be able to keep him in check.

Part of the pro-Trump base sees DeSantis as Trump's spiritual son and holds him in high regard, but many believe his candidacy would represent

---

1 Mary L. Trump, Too Much and Never Enough: How my Family Created the World's Most Dangerous Man, *Editions Simon & Schuster,* July 2020.

2 Ron DeSantis, The Courage to be Free: Florida's Blueprint for America's Revival, Broadside Editions, *Harper Collins Publication,* March 2023, page 66.

a betrayal. The two men seem to have shared a kind of friendship in the years 2018–2020, but today Trump is vindictive. Like an old lion seeing the young guard coming, he's coming out with a few claws based on not-quite-authenticated photos and well-thought-out nicknames. Until now, DeSantis was careful not to fall into Trump's trap and rarely responded to his verbal assaults. When Trump attacked DeSantis as an "average Republican governor with great Public Relations,"[3] DeSantis replied that he, at least, had been re-elected.

At 45, DeSantis could have waited for Trump to leave the political scene before taking his chance later. But in politics, the winds change quickly, and who knows if DeSantis will still be the favorite successor in 2028. Attracted by the challenge, DeSantis took the plunge in 2023, but couldn't defeat his former mentor. He threw in the towel in January 2024.

---

3 Chloé Folmar, Trump Attacks DeSantis Amid Positive Press: "An Average Republican Governor," *The Hill*, November 10, 2022.

CHAPTER 22

DESANTIS'S SUPPORTERS

During his re-election campaign, DeSantis raised over $200 million and received more than 300 six- and seven-figure checks. This is the largest fundraising effort ever by a candidate without his own financing.[1] He did not spend it all, and by early 2023, he was sitting on a war chest of $75 million, to which must be added the seven-figure donations he received in February 2023. While not yet an official candidate, he received $2.5 million from investor/trader Jeffrey Yass and $2 million from the Reyes brothers, billionaires specializing in food distribution.[2]

At the end of February 2023, he organized a fundraising weekend in Palm Beach, Florida, again right next door to Trump's residence. He turned his attention to his wealthy donors, far from the gaze of journalists. According to the *Tallahassee Democrat*, among his biggest donors are some very recognizable names from the Republican establishment:[3] Robert Bigelow, of Bigelow Aerospace, gave him ten million dollars in July 2022. He is one of Florida's major aerospace investors, home to NASA's Cape Canaveral center. Ken Griffin, the head of Citadel, an American investment fund, gave him $5 million to finance his re-election in November 2022, in addition to the $5 million he had already given him for the previous campaign. Other investment fund bosses follow suit, including John W. Childs with $1.3 million, Walter W. Buckley Jr., and Paul Tudor Jones II. Elizabeth and Richard Uihlein, owners

---

1 DeSantis Gains 7-Figure Checks from top GOP Donors, *CBS Miami*, February 22, 2023.

2 Steve Contorno, DeSantis gets 7-figure checks from top GOP donors as he soft launches presidential campaign, *CNN*, February 22, 2023.

3 Zac Anderson, Ron DeSantis has at Least 42 Billionaire Donors, *Tallahassee Democrat*, May 25, 2022.

of the Uline transportation company, gave him a total of $2 million to support his two gubernatorial campaigns.

He is also very close to the wealthy Koch family, of Koch Industries, which founded the powerful conservative association Americans for Prosperity in 2004, with no fewer than 2.3 million members. In 2009, Americans for Prosperity helped the Tea Party become a real political force and opposed Barack Obama's efforts to combat global warming. In 2008, the association circulated a charter entitled "No Climate Tax Pledge," whose signatories pledged to refuse to vote in favor of any kind of federal tax related to climate change. In 2013, a quarter of senators and a third of House representatives signed the pledge. Ron DeSantis was one of them.

Unsurprisingly, the Club for Growth donated $2 million. DeSantis also received more than $10 million from the Republican Governors Association.[4] More surprisingly, the Native American Seminole tribe of Florida who runs the Hard Rock Café franchise in Florida and numerous casinos also gave him $2 million. He also received donations from Julie Fancelli, daughter of the founder of the Floridian supermarket chain Publix; the DeVos family, linked to the co-founder of Amway, a direct sales giant and owner of the Orlando Magic basketball club; and Thomas Peterffy, Florida's richest man. Finally, as already mentioned, DeSantis has the support of the Cuban and Venezuelan communities. While they are important in Florida, this is not the case nationally. Sixty percent of the U.S. Hispanic population originates from Mexico.

In addition to his many financial backers, DeSantis is also backed by Rupert Murdoch, the boss of Fox News and HarperCollins, with whom he signed a lucrative contract to launch his book in February 2023: *Courage to Be Free: Florida's Blueprint to America's Revival*. By then, Rupert Murdoch, the 92-year-old boss of the News Corp empire, was doing everything he could to support his candidate DeSantis, including cutting Donald Trump's airtime, which Trump complained about loudly. After relaying election conspiracy theories in 2020, Fox News was turning against Trump.

Murdoch went even further: he declared under oath in March 2023 that he believed the 2020 election was legitimate and not stolen. He went on to say that

---

4 Zac Anderson, Florida companies dump millions into backdoor fundraising channel for DeSantis, *Tallahassee Democrat*, March 6, 2023.

Donald Trump behaved like a "sore loser."[5] He admitted that his star anchors knowingly lied to viewers by peddling the idea that the 2020 presidential election was rigged. He insisted there was no evidence of this alleged cheating either at the time or subsequently, and the presenters knew that their statements were baseless and misleading. One of the biggest mediatic scandal ever erupted then. Murdoch was shooting down the credibility of his own channel, which is the most watched in the United States and serves as a reference for Republican voters, and was shooting down Trump's claims of rigged elections.

Text exchanges between Tucker Carlson, the channel's star, and a colleague in January 2021 were then revealed:[6] in them, he declared that he couldn't wait to be able to ignore Trump most nights, and he hated him passionately. At the time, however, he was saying the opposite on air, defending Trump's conspiracy theories. His hypocrisy was exposed, and Fox News needed a scapegoat. In April 2023, Tucker Carlson was fired. And all this was really good for Ron DeSantis.

---

5 Ed Pilkington, Stunning Rupert Murdoch Deposition Leaves Fox News in a World of Trouble, *The Guardian*, February 28, 2023.

6 James Gregory, Tucker Carlson said he Hates Trump "Passionately," Lawsuit Reveals, *BBC*, March 8, 2023.

PART 5

DeSantis's America

CHAPTER 23

UNCHECKED GROWTH IN FLORIDA

In a campaign speech, Casey DeSantis pointed out that Florida is now the world's 13th economy.[1] Without taking anything away from DeSantis's political talent, his electoral victory in 2022 is also due to the Florida economic growth on which he is surfing, and which began long before he took office in 2018. As TJ Villamil, Senior Vice President of international trade at Enterprise Florida, told us in January 2023, Florida economic growth is the result of three decades of bipartisan politics.

An agricultural state until the end of the 19th century, Florida's economic development began very late in comparison with the wealthy industrial states of the north. In the 1880s and 1890s, the construction of a railroad linking Florida to the rest of the United States by the visionary industrialist Henry Flagler enabled trade to flourish. In 1890, Flagler began building what he envisioned as the future American Riviera. He founded the cities of Palm Beach (1894) and Miami (1896). The city could have been called "Flagler," but the businessman refused the honor, preferring an ancient name derived from the Native American Indians, Miyaimi.[2]

Tourism slowly emerged, thanks to the mild Floridian climate sought after by chronically ill people with weak bronchi, and to the luxury hotels built by Flagler. But until the 1940s, in popular American imagery, Florida was associated with swamps, mosquitoes, and malaria. It was the most sparsely populated of the southern U.S. states.

In the 1960s, the United States, during the Cold War, embarked on the race to conquer space. The site chosen by NASA for its launchpad was Cape

---

1 Michael Kruze, The Casey DeSantis Problem: "His Greatest Asset and His Greatest Liability," *Politico*, May 19, 2023.

2 Gerald Posner, Miami Babylon, Editions Simon & Schuster, 2009.

Canaveral, on the east coast of Florida. Florida's first economic boom ensued with the arrival of many military personnel and their families, accompanied by the development of technologies essential to the comfort of modern life in Florida (air conditioning in all apartments, refrigerators). Thanks to the widespread use of AC in homes, Florida's population began to grow.

In the 1980s, retirees began to move to Florida, attracted by the climate. At the same time, Florida was plagued by drug cartels and the notorious cocaine cowboys, but the population continued to grow. It was after 2017 that the influx of a more affluent population began to explode, and for one simple reason: Donald Trump's tax reform.

Freshly elected president in 2017, Donald Trump launched a major overhaul of the federal individual and corporate tax system, something that hadn't been done in 30 years. One of the articles of this reform will have an indirect impact on Florida.

Up to 2017, American citizens enjoyed a significant tax advantage: they could deduct the amount of their local taxes from their federal tax return (*SALT deduction* for *State And Local Taxes deduction*) without any capping limit, which was beneficial especially to wealthy tax payers concentrated in California and New York. SALT includes all municipal taxes, as well as income taxes levied by state tax departments. To illustrate, California's income tax rate can be as high as 12.3 percent for the wealthiest households, and up to 10.9 percent in New York.

Trump felt in 2017 that, through this deduction system, States were in a way "stealing" taxes from the federal government, since this was so much money that would not be paid to the IRS. He decided to put an end to this practice and capped the SALT deduction to $10,000. But then, without the deduction, a Californian's or New Yorker's income-tax level became close to 50 percent: the federal rate can rise to 37 percent for the wealthiest incomes, to which must be added the 12.3 percent or 10.9 percent due locally. By virtually putting a stop to this system of local tax deductions, Trump was driving California and New York millionaires and billionaires to other states with more lenient tax regimes.[3]

Meanwhile, Florida, like Texas, had a local income tax of zero. The prospect of saving more than 10 percent in income tax started driving big money to Florida—and Texas. And that's what they've been doing in droves since 2017.

---

3 Chris Edwards, Tax reform and interstate migration, *Cato Institute*, September 6, 2018.

To comply with IRS regulations, these in-migrants spend at least six months and one day in Florida, where they are officially domiciled. The phenomenon is well known in Florida, they are nicknamed the snowbirds.[4] They migrate to Florida in autumn, spend the winter there, then return to New York or other northeastern states in spring and summer. And so it is a migration of wealth that has been settling in Florida since 2017, including many billionaire entrepreneurs from investment funds. In June 2022, Citadel, one of the biggest investment funds in the United States, whose boss is none other than Ken Griffin, one of Ron DeSantis's financial backers, moved its headquarters from Chicago to Miami. Citadel achieved the record for the biggest profit ever made by an investment fund in 2022, with a $16 billion profit in a single year.[5]

This in-migration has intensified since the Covid-19 pandemic. Extremely tough health restrictions in New York and the northeast and midwest states have exhausted the population. At the same time, working remotely has become widely accepted by corporate America. Florida is in the same time zone as New York and is only a three-hour flight away. Geographically, it's an ideal location for New Yorkers working from home. Since 2020, there has been an influx of executives and, more broadly, all types of professions that can be remote.

From 2010 to 2020, Florida's population grew by +15 percent, twice as fast as the rest of the United States, and gained over a million inhabitants in the last three years alone (2020–2023). Florida's total population at the 2020 census was 21.5 million, making it the third most populous state in the United States behind California (39 million) and Texas (29 million). And the growth doesn't stop: Florida's population is predicted to reach 23 million by July 2023.

The demographic boom is beneficial to Florida's economy, where housing is becoming difficult to come by: the real estate market has exploded by +70 percent between 2020 and 2022.[6] The level of education has risen, as have teachers' salaries. Unemployment is only 2.5 percent. According to our interlocutor TJ Villamil, it is commonly said that, since the pandemic, Florida has gained 10 years of growth in two years' time.

---

4 The term also includes Canadians moving to Florida for the winter months.

5 Anna Cooban, Greatest Trade Ever? Citadel's $16 billion Haul Smashes Hedge Fund Records, *CNN*, January 23, 2023.

6 Axel Gylden, Florida, the New Factory of the American Dream, *L'Express*, January 5, 2023.

In addition to agriculture and tourism, Florida's economy is based on the silver economy: between 2010 and 2020, the population aged 65 and over grew by 40 percent and now represents 21 percent of the population, the largest age bracket, closely followed by the 50–65 age group with 20 percent. Logically, the medical network is well-developed and of a high standard.

The economy also relies, more recently—for the past 15 years or so—on exports of high value-added products from the aerospace and aeronautics industries, electronic circuits, and other high-tech products.

Culturally and socially, Florida enjoys a positive image: less sophisticated than California, it is reputed to be friendlier and more welcoming. But we can't talk about Florida without mentioning Miami's international cultural influence:[7] the slightly kitsch city with the sultry reputation of the 1980s has been given a makeover. For over 20 years, the international contemporary art fair Art Basel has positioned the city at the forefront of modern art. Miami is energized: music, design, culinary arts, fashion, the city surfs at the cutting edge of trends. Crime is down sharply. Miami's energetic Republican mayor, Francis X. Suarez intends to make the city the capital of cryptocurrencies and the new home for employees of California's Silicon Valley. Real estate is booming, with three times as many skyscrapers as 10 years ago.

This dynamism is attracting a large French community of nearly 30,000—including 11,500 officially registered with the French Consulate in Miami in 2022. The French population in Florida is expected to grow by 6 percent between 2021 and 2022, ranking Florida fifth among French communities in the United States.[8] While it leans predominantly to the right of the French political spectrum, it is nonetheless diverse: a French restaurant owner specializing in alligator steaks, who has lived in Central Florida for 25 years, told us that "DeSantis is the best, but he has to be patient and wait his turn"; while at the opposite end of the political spectrum, a French biology researcher newly settled in Fort Lauderdale, FL, and an activist for LGBTQ+ rights, told us that "DeSantis is like Donald Trump with a perfect son-in-law face."

While French companies create jobs in every U.S. state, 32,700 jobs were generated by French companies such as Alstom, Framatome, Sodexo,

---

7 Ibid.

8 Laure Pallez, Entretien du 24 mai 2023 avec Laurent Bili Ambassadeur de France aux États-Unis, *Personal Blog*, May 24, 2023.

Air Liquide, Thalès, CMA CGM, and many others in Florida in 2021.[9] The governor's aim is to encourage this trend, to attract even more direct investment (preferably from Europe) and generate skilled jobs in Florida.

We spoke to Franck Bondrille, president-elect of the French Floridian Consular Council. Like many French people in Florida, he believes that the Sunshine State's economic growth is due in large part to its dynamic governor, who favors investment and a lighter pro-business regulatory environment. Under the so-called E2 entrepreneur visa, many French nationals living in Florida have invested a large part of their savings in the purchase of a local American company, and a return to France is no longer an option, whether for financial or personal reasons. For these French people, bankruptcy would mean a compulsory return to France, or at least major administrative problems with the American authorities. Many believe that the survival of numerous French SMEs in Florida during Covid-19 was due to the policies put in place by the governor. The same is true for American SMEs. Many restaurants and other small businesses went bankrupt during the pandemic across the country, unable to survive long lockdowns. It's undeniable that DeSantis's pro-business measures have kept Florida's economy thriving, and even enabled it to overtake other states that have historically been richer and more developed.

---

9 Direction générale du trésor, Rapport économique bilatéral France-USA 2022, April 2002.

CHAPTER 24

DESANTIS'S CAMPAIGN STRATEGY

Make America Florida is the political slogan that DeSantis's teams were beginning to use in early 2023. It echoed the subtitle of Ron DeSantis's book, in which his ambition was clearly expressed: *Florida's blueprint to America's revival.* The term "blueprint" can mean "model" or "construction plan," as the expression is coming from the architect's plans used on a construction site. The idea behind the phrase, then, is to propose using Florida's construction blueprint and replicating it across America to help rebuild a vibrant American economy. And it's going to be complicated.

Florida benefits from an advantageous tax environment, a pleasant climate, a unique coastal location, and is geographically situated at the crossroads of several transportation and communication routes: on the Atlantic side with Europe and North America, and on the Gulf of Mexico side with South America. These ideal conditions seem difficult to duplicate throughout the United States: it is hard to imagine that a central state such as Iowa or Arkansas could one day experience the same economic renaissance as Florida, and that the migration of retirees to sweet Florida would stop and reverse toward the northern states. Some American states are predominantly agricultural, while others suffer from a hostile climate, or even simply unwelcoming terrain: deserts, mountains, glaciers, stretches of agricultural plains. America is known for its geographical diversity. Geography is the primary constraint on people, forging their identity. Not all states are as fortunate as Florida.

Another point that won't be duplicated: Florida's economy exploded thanks to the Covid-19 pandemic, benefiting from the slowdown in all other states. Although possible, the risk of a second global health pandemic happening again soon is low. The development of a significant economic growth gap between U.S. states is unlikely to recur anytime soon.

Additionally, as well known by political leaders and Ron DeSantis, each state has its own legislature and judicial system: it is the master of its own laws and taxation. Even if DeSantis were to become president of the United States, he would have very little room to maneuver and reduce local taxes or regulations to make each state more financially attractive.

What Ron DeSantis really means by Florida's blueprint is that if he's ever elected president of the United States, it's his decisive, direct leadership style that he'll bring with him to the White House, along with his anti-Wokism stance. As he himself states in his book p.250: "The divisions in our society are not merely about different policy preferences regarding taxes, regulations, and welfare, but about our foundational principles." He identifies his battles against "biomedical security state," "stifling woke corporations," and "fighting indoctrination in schools" as his great victories in Florida. Acting quickly and effectively in favor of conservative values is his project for the America of tomorrow.

This is quite a new statement for DeSantis. The fact that he no longer focuses on issues like taxes, regulations, or welfare cuts is edifying. In 2013, then a House representative in Washington, he voted to raise the retirement age and access to free healthcare to 70 years old (currently 67 years old). In 2017, he voted to cut the healthcare budget. Since 2019, he remained silent on these issues. Pressed on the subject, he told Fox News reporter Dana Perino in March 2023:[1] "Look, I have more seniors here [in Florida] than just about anyone as a percentage. You know, we're not going to mess with Social Security as Republicans. I think that that's pretty clear."

DeSantis's political agenda is no longer based on the fiscal conservatism of yesteryear, but now focuses on three areas: (1) a reminder of how he handled the Covid-19 crisis; (2) the fight against the so-called woke corporations; (3) and more broadly, the culture war he wants to replicate across America, principally the fight against CRT in education, the fight against DEI in schools and businesses, and the fight against abortion and limiting the rights of LGBTQ+ communities.

The weight of the first axis of his strategy should not be underestimated: his handling of the pandemic in Florida has not only benefited the economy or the children but also the parents. The fact that Florida's children went back to school as early as the start of the school year in August 2020 was the envy of many across the country. In France and Europe, children returned to school before the end of the school year, around May 2020. This return of children

---

1 Yacob Reyes, Rep. Ron DeSantis Backed Raising Social Security and Medicare Age; Gov. DeSantis has Different Tack, *Politifact*, March 15, 2023.

to the classroom was consensual in French society, as it was vital not only for children's education and development, but also for the economy by enabling parents to return to the workplace. In the United States, the situation varied greatly from state to state.

A mother from Illinois testifies:

"My children, then aged 7 and 8, were unable to attend school from March 2020 to January 2021. They went to school from home, each locked in their own room from 8am to 2.30pm, excluding lunch breaks, on IPads provided by the school administration. After some initial difficulties, the children quickly became experts on their tablets, then gradually developed a form of screen addiction, especially as they had homework to do at the end of the day on the IPads and unlimited access to an online bookstore. They were doing between 7 and 8 hours of screen time a day. In December 2020, still no communication from the school, so I decided to take part in a demonstration organized by parents to demand the children's return to school. The situation was all the more frustrating because the private schools had already reopened since August 2020! At the end of January 2021, face-to-face school finally resumed, but on a part-time basis: children attended from 12:00 to 2:30 pm. It was better than nothing, but still very limited. With the teacher busy all day in class with the morning half-group and then the afternoon half-group, the children were "on their own" for the rest of the school day, having to work independantly on their screens. It was only for the last two months of the school year, April and May 2021, that they returned to school full-time, i.e. a year after the start of the pandemic. That year was a difficult time for our family. The children didn't suffer academically, but rather mentally because of the lack of socialization with their classmates, and my mental balance suffered too."

American cities in which schools were closed had Covid-19 rates identical to those with open schools, whether in the United States or Europe. In October 2022, "Maths and reading levels were all lower than normal this fall," explains David Leonhardt from *the New York Times*.[2] The effects of school closures have been particularly felt in disadvantaged, black, and Latino communities. Depression rates have risen, and the American Pediatric Association has declared October 2021 a national emergency for children's mental health, with increased admissions to psychiatric emergency departments.

---

2 David Leonhardt, No Way to Grow Up, *The New York Times*, January 4, 2022.

Teachers' unions in large school districts such as New York, Chicago, and Los Angeles have forced school districts to be cautious about Covid-19. Strongly rooted on the left, teachers' unions became the target of right-wing politicians in early 2021, who accused them of "faucism," claiming schools prioritized the health of teachers over that of children.[3]

DeSantis often recalls what he did in Florida to get kids back to school and pledges to fight the power of unions. This is likely to resonate with many parents, especially those American women who were forced to stay at home for a year, the *rage moms* who protested school closures. This female electorate could be convinced by the common sense put into action by Ron DeSantis.

Its second axis, fighting woke corporatism, can be broken down in two ways: obviously, the first is the fight against companies that too openly promote LGBTQ+ rights, such as Disney. Other recent examples: Budweiser Light beers had to withdraw their partnership with a transsexual influencer; the M&M's brand had to remove its famous colorful round characters after unwittingly creating controversy by trying to give them less gendered, more sensitive attributes. In fact, large American companies are increasingly encouraged to take a political stand by their consumers and employees. However, these political boycotts go both ways in the United States: in 2020, the canned vegetable brand Goya suffered a boycott after its CEO publicly complimented Donald Trump; in 2022, the music platform Spotify also came under pressure from artists and users who threatened to leave the site until the podcast by the controversial Joe Rogan, accused of spreading false information about the Covid-19 vaccine, was suspended.[4]

The second way of fighting woke corporatism is to go after those who are openly advocating for the climate and trying to reduce their carbon footprint, and more generally, those who claim to have an environmental, social, and governance (ESG) policy, either in favor of the environment, social policies, or better governance.

The acronym ESG has a positive connotation in Europe, but in the United States, it has become in just a few months the new whipping boy of conservatives, who denounce any attempt to change consumer behavior through ESG policies. Microsoft bore the brunt of this in January 2023: as they

---

3 David Leonhardt, The Long Shadow of Covid School Closures, *The New York Times*, April 28, 2023.

4 Peniel E. Joseph, Don't pretend you don't know what Joe Rogan is all about, *CNN*, February 10, 2022.

announced the launch of an Xbox console that would consume less electricity and have a smaller carbon footprint, they were immediately accused by some Republicans and Fox News journalists of playing environmentalist politics and trying to recruit gamers to their cause from an early age.[5]

Similarly, the bankruptcy of Silicon Valley Bank in March 2023 was immediately attributed by Ron DeSantis to the liberal woke management of its board, which would have done better to concentrate on traditional business.[6] While the reasons for the failure can be attributed at worst to governance errors, but not to the investments made by the bank, the message getting through is that banks that seek to adopt ESG principles fail, and ESG businesses will cause a downturn in the economy.

To underline his stance and seriousness, Ron DeSantis withdrew two billion dollars of Florida state assets from the BlackRock investment fund, to sanction the latter for adopting ESG policies and a governance deemed too progressive.[7] On the same note, Florida pension fund managers are now prohibited from taking ESG criteria into account in their financial investment decisions.

This anti-ESG strategy will speak to a conservative or even moderate electorate in favor of the free-market economy and against pro-environment regulations.

The third axis of his campaign strategy is the culture war. We've already seen how DeSantis has succeeded in imposing his conservative values on all strata of Floridian society. To do the same at the national level, he relies on a few strong statements, such as "Freedom of expression does not include the right to indoctrinate," but he will also emphasize the supposed excesses of wokism which should be countered.

With objectivity, we must point out that in the United States, some states have gone very far in promoting CRT and DEI, to the point of annoying a section of the population. A mother in Washington, DC, tells us that the story of Rosa Parks is taught every year in elementary school. While Rosa Parks is an important figure in U.S. history, the repeated teaching could be perceived as politically motivated. Another controversial example: one of the

---

5 Alexander Hall, Xbox becomes first "carbon aware" console, but not everyone is happy: "Woke brigade is after video games," *Fox News*, January 23, 2023.

6 Sam Sutton, Silicon Valley Bank gets a Spin on the Anti-ESG Turntable, *Politico*, March 15, 2023.

7 Sarah Halifa-Legrand, Florida, America's Ultraconservative Laboratory, *L'Obs*, January 19, 2023.

school academies in the heavily Democrat state of Vermont (home state of Bernie Sanders) stated in an April 2023 directive that the terms "boy" and "girl" would be replaced by "person who produces sperm" and "person who produces eggs" in a course on the reproductive system and puberty for fifth graders. This decision, supported by the school's parents, was taken in the interests of inclusion for all children whatever their sexual orientation, and might be somehow perceived as excessive.

Another thought-provoking topic: to "protect" transgender children from parents who might not always be kind to them, some educators and faculty members are going to great lengths. In September 2020, a Florida mother filed a complaint against the practices of her 13-year-old daughter's middle school board.[8]

The family had discussed their daughter's desire for gender transition with her. The parents had refused to let her take a male first name but had allowed her to use a nickname of her choice at school. However, the educators, psychologists, and school management, together with the child and without informing the parents, drew up a gender transition plan for the child, including changing her first name and pronoun on the school campus and using the toilets of the opposite sex. The parents' complaint is that they have been excluded from all discussions. The school administration refused to share with them the transition plan and any updates on the situation and encouraged the young teenager not to talk to their parents about it, thus placing them in the position of the enemy. It is easy to understand the parents' dismay at being excluded from such an intimate and complex subject, affecting the well-being of a young child.

These few examples show that the quest for racial, social, and gender fairness and inclusion can generate complicated situations that are open to interpretation and can be debated by both sides of the political spectrum. DeSantis sees them as great excesses that should be remedied.

---

8 Andrew Atterbury and Gary Fineout, How a Lawsuit over a Teen Spurred Florida Republicans to Pass the "Don't Say Gay" Law, *Politico*, March 29, 2022.

CHAPTER 25

DESANTIS'S AMERICA

In Ronald Reagan's time, the Republican Party was the party of free trade, businessmen, and unbridled capitalism. Is it now becoming the party of the middle class?

DeSantis is targeting the hard-working middle class, wage earners, and small business owners. *Main street, not Wall street:*[1] this expression reflects his position on the economy. He wants to lead for the middle class from which he comes, and he claims a form of independence from big corporations. Real or supposed independence, it's true that he has opposed the sugar lobby, the BlackRock investment fund, Disney, and the big pharmaceutical companies. But the powerful financial backing he enjoys for his campaign undoubtedly comes with a quid pro quo. What kind of president would he be? What would he try to put in place?

DeSantis believes deeply in American exceptionalism, in the Judeo-Christian tradition, and in the existence of inalienable rights granted by God to man—and superior to the rights that men grant each other. Inspired by the *NatCons* (nationalist-conservatives), his economic program is one of retrenchment and protectionism, marked by an anti-ESG crusade. While he would probably continue Biden's efforts and his infrastructure investment plan, we could expect priority to be given to projects that create skilled jobs, but not to projects that save energy or combat global warming.

On immigration, DeSantis has often spoken out in favor of building a wall on the U.S.-Mexico border and deporting undocumented migrants. In terms of security and public order, he favors a strong, muscular stance. He argues

---

1 Flore Kayl and Laure Pallez, "United States: Is the Republican Party Becoming the Party of the Middle Class?", *Marianne*, February 13, 2023.

that Democrat and Woke states have never succeeded in reducing crime and insecurity.

Another topic: if elected, DeSantis could ask members of the House to set up a corruption commission against Joe Biden's son Hunter, who is suspected of receiving money from a Chinese company linked to the Communist Party and a Ukrainian natural gas company.[2]

If DeSantis takes a less fiscally conservative line than in the past, he would surely try to reduce funding for the powerful federal agencies he dislikes. He often referred to the "power of the purse" philosophy, which allows the U.S. Congress to reduce the funding and "nuisance" power of certain federal branches of government, such as the IRS and the CDC. While not wishing to shut down federal agencies altogether, he would reduce their workforce in the hope of making them more efficient. We could therefore expect layoffs in many government departments, especially education.[3] DeSantis distrusts bureaucratic experts. He believes that they predict the worst-case scenarios without ever proving their claims, and that they are often wrong without ever admitting it afterward. In this regard, he highlights several examples in his book: in 2003, to justify the invasion of Iraq, foreign policy experts claimed the presence of weapons of mass destruction, but this was never subsequently proven; in 2017, diplomatic experts and the American secret service predicted a geopolitical disaster in Israel if the American embassy moved from Tel Aviv to Jerusalem, and nothing of the sort happened; in 2020, the response to the Covid-19 pandemic by the experts failed to take into account the damage done by a strict health policy to the American economy and mental health, particularly that of children. Overall, he believes that the bureaucratic elite is unreliable and disappears in important moments. No doubt he would also attempt to cut funding for medical and scientific experts. If he becomes president one day, he wouldn't trust them, which could prove problematic, particularly in his response to the global warming crisis.

DeSantis has a rather bleak view of America: "The Democrats consider us to be subjects to be ruled over. They don't consider us to be on equal footing with them. They think we should bow down to their ideology,"[4] he said, during

---

2 Hunter Biden: What was he Doing in China and Ukraine?, *BBC*, April 6, 2021.

3 Interview with John Stossel, The Full Interview on 2024, Donald Trump, COVID, the Border Crisis, Education & More, *YouTube*, May 23, 2023.

4 Gabriel Sherman, Ron DeSantis, the Making and Remaking (and Remaking) of a MAGA Heir, *Vanity Fair*, September 27, 2022.

a speech in Pittsburgh. There's no doubt that, as president, his attention would turn to the societal issues we mentioned earlier: restricting abortion rights, access to gender-change therapy and drag shows; expanding access to firearms; animosity with the mainstream media and a return to the rhetoric of *fake news*. DeSantis is more disciplined and hard-working than Trump, so he would get more done and get on with the job without delay.

These societal issues are fundamental, and we could expect American society to be as divided as it has been under the Trump presidency. The risk of a "cold civil war"—a civil war without armed conflict between Republican and Democrat states as imagined by the influential conservative political theorist Angelo Codevilla—is real. America today would be even more divided than it was during the Civil War, he says, for once Americans at least shared a common faith in the same God.[5]

In the United States, the concept of equality between men, regardless of race or gender, is complex. There are three words that overlap but cover different concepts: *Equality, Equity,* and *Fairness*. All the laws passed in Florida allowing gender-based discrimination would be invalidated if a federal law guaranteeing equality between all men in the broadest sense, all humans whatever their gender identity and sexual orientation, existed in the United States. However, this is not the case.

The law currently in force is the Civil Rights Act of 1964, which prohibits discrimination based on race, color, religion, sex, or national origin. It prohibits discrimination in access to voting, in schools and public transport, and in hiring. The law needs to be modernized to take account of changes in society, and Biden made a new Equality Act one of his campaign planks for 2020. On the very first day of his presidency, he signed an executive order prohibiting discrimination based on gender transition and sexual orientation. While the Supreme Court has issued several rulings against transgender discrimination in recent years, LGBTQ+ rights may still be considered as fragile in the United States, and an executive order can easily be overturned by the next administration. Democrats would like to see the Equality Act passed definitively.

Within weeks of taking office, Joe Biden pushed the Equality Act to the floor of the House of Representatives, and it passed; but since then, it stalled in the Senate. On the other hand, even if it ever passed in the Senate, it would surely be blocked by the federal Supreme Court. Explanations: in 2017, a

---

5 Angelo M. Codevilla, The Cold Civil War, *Claremont Review of Books*, 2017.

Californian baker refused to make a wedding cake for a couple of homosexual women, justifying his refusal by his religious values, which ran counter to gay marriage. The subject is legally complex. In 2022, the cake-maker won his case and set a precedent. The Religious Freedom Restoration Act of 1993 thus took precedence over any existing—or future—laws in favor of equal treatment of genders and against discrimination based on sexual orientation. Such legal loopholes can easily be exploited by a government on a mission to return to a conservative, heteronormative vision of the family.

In a context of extreme political tension in the United States, the role of the federal Supreme Court is all-powerful. Theoretically, the Supreme Court is the guardian of the temple on these issues, but today is it still a neutral judicial body, or has it become a political one? If the justices use their power to the full by transforming themselves into lifelong members of an unelected third chamber, the Supreme Court risks losing its ability to be the ultimate decision-maker, a role it was asked to play in the 2000 presidential election—and again in 2020. Let's not forget that, in the 2000 presidential election, it was the Supreme Court's conservative majority that gave George W. Bush victory, by stopping the recount of votes in Florida.

In the long term, the question of the legitimacy of the Supreme Court goes beyond the question of abortion rights or the protection of minorities by law. If state laws were to diverge so widely that no one in California could own a firearm and homosexuals in Texas were not allowed anymore to adopt children, each state would have a profoundly different value base. This would lead to migratory movements within the country. We'd be on the verge of national disintegration.

The French *L'Obs* magazine[6] of January 19, 2023, tells the story of Alex Ingram, a white teacher from Jacksonville, Florida, who has just resigned to move to another state. He feels he can no longer teach African American history according to his values. Every day, he receives threats and runs the risk of having his teaching license suspended. With tears in his eyes, he says he must leave and head to a state where he can teach without censorship.

Similarly, according to a study published in January 2023 by the Williams Institute,[7] which surveyed 113 parents of LGBTQ+ children in Florida, 56

---

6 Sarah Halifa Legrand, America's Ultraconservative Laboratory, *L'Obs*, January 19, 2023.

7 Impact of HB1557 (Florida's Don't Say Gay bill) on LGBTQ+ Parents in Florida, *Williams Institute, UCLA School of Law,* January 2023.

percent of them are considering leaving Florida because they fear an increase in harassment toward their children and a hardening of public policies against the community. Like NBA player Dwyane Wade of the Miami Heats, who announced in April 2023 that he was leaving Florida and moving with his family, to protect his transgender daughter from the anxiety-inducing and potentially dangerous political climate.

While the possibility of massive in-migration between states still seems remote, and the scenario of a cold civil war between Democrat and Republican states remains unlikely, it is nevertheless urgent for the U.S. Supreme Court to rediscover its role as a balanced arbiter and the path of compromise.[8]

It's worth noting that the polarization of American political life is leading to excesses and increasing violence against political figures of all stripes. In November 2022, the husband of Nancy Pelosi, then Democrat Speaker of the House, was attacked at his home by a right-wing extremist. In April 2023, the home of a Republican senator from Utah was vandalized, in response to a bill he was trying to pass against gender-change therapy for minors. When violence takes the place of dialogue, it's democracy that is at risk and weakened.

---

8 Laure Pallez and Florence Baillon, Le droit à l'interruption volontaire de grossesse : un chemin à géométrie variable, *Think Tank la France et le Monde en Commun*, May 2022.

CHAPTER 26

FOREIGN AFFAIRS

Ron DeSantis's vision of international relations was shaped by his years in the army and his position on the Foreign Affairs Committee when he was a House representative in Washington.

His rare statements on foreign policy have two characteristics: they are more conventional than those of Donald Trump, even if he still uses national-conservative language against globalization and the elites in his speeches; they also reflect, logically enough, the concerns of his Florida voters. As far as Latin America is concerned, we saw he is markedly hostile to the governments of Cuba, Venezuela, and Colombia. Florida has the fourth largest Jewish community in the United States, behind New York, California, and New Jersey, with around 650,000 people. DeSantis is a fervent supporter of Israel, having pledged to be "America's most pro-Israel governor."

Although he has always voted in favor of increasing the U.S. defense budget, he does not support state interventionism. However, he does see military power as strategic, mainly as a deterrent. This defensive stance is in line with that of Ronald Reagan and the opposite of the neo-conservatives of the George W. Bush era. In his inaugural address right after he was invested president of the United States, President Bush declared: "The survival of liberty in our land increasingly depends on the success of liberty in other lands."[1] DeSantis is opposed to this position, opposing on principle any American intervention on foreign soil, as in 2013 when Barack Obama wanted to intervene in Syria. He considers such operations too costly in human and financial terms and not essential to maintaining American freedom. Although he was in favor of the American intervention against the Talibans and Al Qaeda, considered necessary and legitimate after the attacks of September 11, 2001, he wanted

---

1 George W. Bush, Inaugural address, January 20, 2005.

the troops to return home after their mission had been successfully completed, rather than be involved in the project to consolidate democracy in Afghanistan. And indeed, the chaotic withdrawal of American troops from Afghanistan in 2021 and the return of the Talibans to power are a reminder of the immense difficulty of such a task.

DeSantis is also strongly opposed to the Iranian regime and the civilian nuclear program negotiated by Obama and canceled by Trump. He is also opposed to China, which he considers a powerful enemy. He supports the idea that we need to stand firm against these two countries and weaken them economically, especially China.

As governor of Florida, he has adopted a series of measures to limit Chinese investment in the Sunshine State. Florida companies with sales more than $100,000 must declare any commercial links with China. Like many other American states, DeSantis banned Confucius Institutes from the campuses of Florida's public universities. This Chinese organization, officially dedicated to promoting international educational partnerships, is considered a propaganda organ affiliated with the Chinese Communist Party (CCP).

DeSantis is also invested in security issues concerning the CCP, to protect Florida's booming high-tech and aerospace sectors. In 2022, a Chinese company purchased farmland adjacent to an air base in North Dakota. Concerned that this could happen in Florida, DeSantis pushed a law in 2023 prohibiting companies and individuals from seven blacklisted countries— China, of course, but also Venezuela, Cuba, Russia, Iran, North Korea, and Syria—from acquiring land around Florida military bases, as well as farmland. In early 2023, the DeSantis administration offered a $25 million package to police forces so that they could replace their made-in-China drones with American ones. Mobile applications such as TikTok (owned by a Chinese conglomerate) are banned from the servers of Florida's schools and administrative buildings. Public universities are prohibited from receiving any form of Chinese funding or gifts.

According to Walter Mead, a world-renowned expert, there are four main currents of thought in American foreign policy, inspired by the American presidents who defined them.[2] The Hamiltonians, like Bill Clinton, believe that American interests, particularly commercial interests, should be at the heart of foreign policy. They see commercial capitalism as a tool for peace and

---

2 Walter Mead, *Special Providence: American Foreign Policy and How It Changed the World*, Routledge, 2002.

constitute the majority school of thought in Washington. Wilsonians, like the neo-conservative George W. Bush, believe that promoting liberal democracy abroad serves American security interests. Jeffersonians, on the other hand, favor geographic expansion and free trade, and the maintenance of a democratic global system.

These three camps have been challenged in recent decades—and particularly since Trump's presidential election—by the rise of a Jacksonian or populist vision of world politics, from which DeSantis seems to draw inspiration. According to this current, the world is the site of a struggle between competitors, whether in politics or economics. Jacksonians fear that the American people will lose this competition because of their over-reliance on the global economy. Lower-middle-class workers would be the hardest hit, as they have seen production relocate and international competition intensify.

In foreign policy, the sentiment expressed by Jacksonians is first and foremost that of a warrior nationalism, ready to defend itself in the face of any attack, but hostile to bloodshed for democracy, skeptical about the responsibility and even the possibility of the United States preserving an international order. The United States must defend its honor abroad by relying on powerful allies like Europe and Japan, remain vigilant and armed but with the sole aim of protecting its own vital interests, such as energy supplies or a specific geostrategic advantage. Typically, a Jacksonian won't promote democratic elections in a country if the result of the elections brings an anti-American government to power.

This is in line with NatCon ideas: military interest in NATO is low, and the European Union is seen more as a trading partner—if not an adversary— with whom it is difficult to do business because of hyper-regulation of safety and environmental standards, to which Americans are not yet sensitive. Furthermore, each European country has abdicated part of its sovereignty (currency, borders, law) in favor of a supranational organization, which the NatCon movement views negatively: the movement advocates sovereignty, specifically the sovereignty of the United States, and protests interference from foreign powers.

In a speech entitled "Florida versus Davos," which he delivered at the 3rd NatCon conference[3] in September 2022, DeSantis declared that the United States is a nation that has an economy, not the other way around: "Our

---

3 Speech delivered at the National Conservatism Conference, September 2022, Miami, transcript available on the American Mind website.

economy should be geared toward helping our own people," he said. Some criticize him for going beyond the Trumpist "America first" stance and being almost "America only."

However, the ever-pragmatic DeSantis is not an extremist: he is neither an isolationist nor a "globalist." Rather, DeSantis is a realist, focused on U.S. interests at home, or abroad if U.S. interests are threatened there. The American president who best represents this foreign policy is Ronald Reagan, who fought Russian influence in South America and Europe by all possible means, notably in Poland with the help of Pope John Paul II, and who backed out of an international arms control treaty on the grounds that it was not in America's favor. Ron DeSantis is a great admirer of the former Republican president and quotes him often in his autobiographical book.

Regarding Ukraine, DeSantis remains on the sidelines and avoids making a statement unless he is forced to do so. He seems to have no clear position on the subject. While he was in favor of a firm policy against Putin in 2017, declaring that the latter was trying to rebuild the Russian empire of yesteryear, lately he seems less assertive. In early 2023, he declared in an interview on Fox News: "I don't think it's in our interests to get into a proxy war against China over the borders of Ukraine or Crimea."[4] By believing that the conflict could be summed up as a "territorial dispute," he incurred the wrath of the Republican Party establishment, for whom the war in Ukraine represented an unacceptable attack on America's dominant position in the world. As Tara Varma, a researcher fellow at the Brookings Institution in Washington, explained to us in an interview in May 2023, Republicans once again believe in "reincarnating the greatness of America."

Backtracking a few weeks later, DeSantis asserted in March 2023 that Russia's invasion of Ukraine is obviously to be condemned, and that Putin is a war criminal who must be held accountable for his actions. He also maintained that America must not send troops to Ukraine or increase its military support—which is already substantial.

Russia's economic power, apart from its military might, is like that of Italy. Russia cannot compete with the American economy, unlike China, whose economic weight is close to that of the United States. What's interesting about DeSantis' comment on Ukraine is the idea of a "proxy war" with China.

China is more worrying than Russia in Washington, and this concern is bipartisan. Commercially, China is fast and technologically advanced,

---

4 David Brooks, Let's All do the DeSantis Shimmy!, *New York Times*, February 23, 2023.

particularly in the solar panel and Artificial Intelligence sectors. In fact, Trump was the first American president to warn of the danger posed by China's economic power and to adopt restrictive import measures. According to the *Wall Street Journal*,[5] Europeans are reluctant to follow the Americans in their trade conflict with China. Emmanuel Macron's position at the beginning of 2023 is highly irritating to the Americans: a trade partnership between France and China is the very opposite of what the Americans want, which is namely to "contain" the expansion of the Chinese economy.

On the military front, China's aggressive weapons policy is even more worrying. The United States has a stockpile of around 3,750 nuclear warheads, compared with 6,000 for Russia, a significant proportion of which is in poor working order (for comparison, France has 290). At best, the United States can produce between 50 and 80 nuclear warheads a year. Chinese president Xi Jinping's stated aim is to surpass the United States militarily within the next 30 years, or around 2050. In an article for *The Hill*,[6] Matthew R. Costlow, an analyst at the National Institute of Public Policy, highlights the faster-than-expected increase in China's nuclear arsenal. In 2020, the US Department of Defense estimated that China would reach a stockpile of 400 nuclear warheads by 2030, a serious underestimate as China reached 400 warheads in just one year, in 2021.[7]

In a May 2023 interview with Emily Benson, a researcher at CSIS (Center for Strategic and International Studies) in Washington, Benson mentioned the United States no longer has a human intelligence presence in China, so it's hard to know what's going on there. Moreover, diplomatic relations with China have been very sporadic between February and May 2023 since the spy balloon affair.[8] Biden called on China to forge closer ties as soon as possible at the G7 meeting in May 2023 and welcomed Xi Jinping in San Francisco in November 2023. It was under the Biden administration, however, that controls on U.S. exports to China were increased, amid fears that American technologies sent to Chinese individuals or companies might fall directly into

---

5 Laurence Norman and Austin Ramzi, China Seeks to Pry Europe Away From Washington, *Wall Street Journal*, May 10, 2023.

6 Matthew Coslow, Does China Want Nuclear Superiority?, *The Hill*, January 24, 2023.

7 Flore Kayl and Laure Pallez, États-Unis—Chine, la tension monte, Fondation Jean-Jaurès, March 2, 2023.

8 Ibid.

the hands of the Chinese People's Liberation Army. A position which alerts Beijing to American intentions and sincerity.

At the same time, Biden's stated objectives for the U.S. production chain are clear: it's no longer a question of *decoupling* the U.S. economy from China, but of *derisking* (limiting exposure to risk). According to Emily Benson, after the pandemic-related shortage, it was urgent to think of a plan B and find suppliers outside China for four ultra-strategic business sectors: pharmaceuticals (China is a leading producer of cancer drugs, for example), rare minerals, batteries, and semiconductors.[9] The idea of *re-shoring* to the United States runs up against the reality on the ground: when Taiwanese company TSMC tried to open the doors of its first factory in Arizona, it faced a low-skilled American workforce and a lack of water. The project is currently making slow progress.

The United States is looking for reliable partners elsewhere and is keen to replicate the *frontiering* model implemented by IBM in Japan. The company was able to establish itself in the land of the rising sun by forming a coalition with the Japanese government, a long-standing and reliable American ally. Since then, the Americans have set their sights on similar partnerships in Southeast Asia, including Indonesia, South Korea, and Malaysia. The partnering countries must have a skilled workforce and stable power supply, essential to manufacturing high-tech microchips.

According to French historian and researcher Dr. Maya Kandel, author of the blog *Froggy Bottom*, in an interview with us in May 2023, China is the United States' most important bilateral relationship, and therefore the one with the greatest potential impact on the future world order. And while it's true that one doesn't always choose one's enemy, it seems clear that China has chosen hers: the United States. A common expression in Washington is the "G2": ultimately, global geopolitics revolve around these two great powers, even if the other forces at play are not negligible.

Xi Jinping's reckless approach to Taiwan is therefore extremely worrying. Taiwan is far more strategic for the United States than Ukraine, as they have been militarily engaged with Taiwan since the early 1950s. A mutual defense treaty in the event of military aggression has existed between the two countries since 1954. Moreover, Taiwan is perceived as an important geopolitical barrier: it is at the center of the "First Island Chain," a strategic barrier of

---

9 Flore Kayl and Laure Pallez, De l'influence des nationaux-conservateurs sur la politique étrangère et économique des États-Unis, think tank La France et le monde en commun, June 2023.

Westernized islands in the western Pacific that includes the Philippines, Indonesia, Vietnam, and Japan. According to Dr. Maya Kandel, the fall of Taiwan would have disastrous consequences for the American economy. Emily Benson confirms: Taiwanese company TSMC currently produces 98 percent of the world's advanced chips. What's more, if Taiwan falls into Chinese hands, it could unbalance the entire Southeast Asian region.[10]

To boost his international profile, DeSantis toured Japan, South Korea, Israel, and the United Kingdom in April 2023. In the choice of countries he visited, DeSantis showed little interest in the European Union. In an interview with Japan,[11] he acknowledged that China is determined to take back Taiwan, stressing that "Ultimately, what China respects is strength," implying that China respects the military power of the United States. DeSantis's position on Taiwan is clear: America has nothing to gain from an armed conflict with China over the Taiwan question. He adds: "The goal should be to deter a military situation from happening." Massive investment by the U.S. military will therefore be required to counter the Chinese arms race, and to maintain America's current superiority in numbers and technology. As he reiterated in an interview with John Stossel in May 2023:[12] his foreign policy strategy can be summed up as "Peace through strength."

As Tara Varma reminds us, Obama was already stressing in 2009 at the COP in Copenhagen that, although historical Western allies such as Europe are committed to the American cause and are reliable, they must learn to defend themselves alone, and this position is widely shared today in Washington, even more so in regards to the war in Ukraine.

Tara Varma also points out that there is widespread concern in the capital: the United States—like the Europeans—have sent a significant proportion of their weaponry to Ukraine, and they will certainly never see it again, leaving them both weakened in the event of a direct attack. That said, a war in Ukraine is a land war, whereas a war in Taiwan would be a sea war, which does not correspond to the same armament requirements. One thing is certain, she tells us: "Until five years ago, there was a technological rivalry with China; today, the possibility of a conflict with China has become very real."

---

10 Francis Sempa, The Difference Between Ukraine and Taiwan, *The Diplomat*, January 31, 2022.

11 Republican Hopeful DeSantis backs Taiwan Deterrence, *France 24*, April 25, 2023.

12 Ron DeSantis—The Full Interview on 2024, Donald Trump, COVID, the Border Crisis, Education & More, *YouTube*, May 23, 2023.

   DeSantis concluded his interview in Japan by declaring that Europe must do more for Ukraine if the United States is to concentrate on threats to Taiwan. In so doing, he defined the roles of each of the two great historical allies. As Dr. Maya Kandel reminds us, DeSantis has no firm position or ideology on foreign policy. While he would refocus U.S. foreign policy on the Western Hemisphere, DeSantis is a realist focused on U.S. interests. It is likely that his positions will evolve in the months and years to come in line with developments in world geopolitics.

CHAPTER 27

FLORIDA IN 2023

On March 7, 2023, Florida's parliamentary session for the year 2023 opened. It was held in Tallahassee, the capital of the Sunshine State for 60 days. As soon as the session opened, Ron DeSantis gave a lengthy speech to Florida's elected representatives, reaffirming his positions: the tone was one of hardening. Followed by a supportive Florida House and Senate, he carried out his program, and numerous laws were quickly passed and signed into law by DeSantis in April and May 2023:

Abortion is no longer permitted beyond six weeks of pregnancy, except in cases of rape. The onus is on the victim to provide proof of rape. In less than two years, Florida has gone from a 25-week abortion ban to a 6-week ban.

Weapons can now be purchased without a permit or background check, and concealed weapons can be carried in public places, such as supermarkets.

In the spring of 2023, the Don't Say Gay law was extended to eighth graders. All programs promoting Diversity, Equality, and Inclusion are canceled in public universities. Unions representing civil servants, including teachers, must have at least 60 percent of employees in their ranks, which will greatly hamper their very existence.[1] If they are made up of less than 60 percent employees, they will lose their certification as a union and their place at the bargaining table with school district boards. A total of 45 teachers' and administrative staff unions would be affected. This latest law is being challenged in the courts.

To leave parents free to choose the education they wish for their children, the State of Florida is increasing the number of school vouchers allocated to families wishing to enroll their children in private schools. Home-schooled children, as well as children attending charter schools or magnet schools, will

---

1 Emma Behrmann, Florida Senate Passes Bill that Would Undermine Most of State's Teacher Unions, *WGCU*, March 30, 2023.

also be eligible for these vouchers. The maximum allowance is $7,800 per child per school year. This does not cover the full cost of tuition for private schools, but it should help some families to take the plunge and send their children to a private school or take them out of the public curriculum. In 2022, approximately 400,000 Floridian students attend private schools, and this figure is expected to rise. Comparatively, there are a bit less than three million public school students in Florida.

On May 17, 2023,[2] DeSantis signed a law called Let Kids Be Kids prohibiting public funding of gender-change drug therapies for minors; the law bans pronoun and gender changes and the use of restrooms that don't match a child's biological sex in schools; the law also aims to reduce drag shows.

The immigration law signed by DeSantis in May 2023 tightens conditions for undocumented migrants in Florida, hoping to deter and reduce the influx of immigrants. Owners of private companies with more than 25 employees are required to register all their employees on the federal E-Verify online platform, including the previously exempt agricultural sector, hotels, restaurants, and construction, all of which are in high demand for immigrant labor. The expected unofficial boomerang effect of this measure is that undocumented workers will probably still be working illegally but companies will no longer pay taxes on wages paid, as was the case until now. This will generate less tax revenue for the Florida government. It should also be noted that the difficulty of finding legal workers in agriculture could lead to higher food prices. Another anti-immigration measure: workers whose driver's license is from another state can no longer use it to get hired in Florida: all Floridian workers will have to have an ID made in Florida. This set of rules voted in the spring of 2023, which is not described here in exhaustive detail, is very strict, among the most restrictive in the United States.

We've already mentioned the laws against nationals of seven blacklisted countries, including the Chinese, who can no longer buy farmland or land near a Florida military site.

As for the death penalty—which exists in Florida for aggravated murder—a new law attempts to extend it to criminals guilty of raping a child under the age of 12. This is the first time the death penalty would be applied for a non-murder crime in Florida, and it would run counter to previous rulings by the

---

2 DeSantis Signs Bills Targeting Drag Shows, Transgender Kids and the Use of Bathrooms and Pronouns, *US News*, May 17, 2023.

U.S. Supreme Court. It is therefore unlikely that this law will see the light of day. It is challenged in courts.

On the economic front, the state is benefiting from population growth and sales-tax revenues (capped at 7.5 percent). The budget for the year 2023 amounts to a record $113 billion, enabling all projects to be financed and even reserves to be maintained. All state employee salaries are increased by 5 percent. In response to Florida's housing crisis, the government will invest over a billion dollars in the construction of low-income housing. To combat inflation, a number of sales-tax exemptions are passed on baby products or the cost of private day-care centers, for example; at the same time, other laws have been voted on that open the door to increases in insurance policies, and water and electricity bills. Another law will strictly regulate the lawsuits that can be brought against insurance companies, protecting them from far-fetched lawsuits. Other measures have been passed to reduce the cost of medicines and provide access to social security for as many needy children as possible.

Finally, a few other laws are more anecdotal but just as revealing: local municipalities no longer have the right to prohibit the use of fertilizers during the rainy season. Teachers have the right to confiscate students' cell phones.

Overall, DeSantis won just about every piece of legislation he'd hoped to pass, except two: a bill that would have made it easier for him to sue the media for defamation; and another that would have stripped the children of immigrants who grew up in Florida—the Dreamers—of the right to preferential college rates at Florida universities.

This legislative session is therefore seen as a success for the Republicans and DeSantis. Additional laws were passed that reinforce his executive power and authority. The State Guard is to be tripled in size, and its budget has increased tenfold. For the first time in Florida, travel by the governor and other elected officials is now protected and will no longer be made public. In addition, a new law tailor-made for DeSantis allows the governor to remain in office even if he is a presidential candidate, which was not the case before. Finally, another law retroactively legalizes the sending of undocumented migrants to Martha's Vineyard. All the elements are in place to guarantee the success of the official announcement of his candidacy for the presidential election. And this he finally did on May 24, 2023, alongside Elon Musk, on the social networking platform Twitter (now X).

The choice of relying on X is an interesting one: despite some technical problems encountered at the start of the connection, X gives Ron DeSantis a modern image. What's more, Twitter was an important tool in Donald Trump's 2016 campaign strategy: the network is a good vehicle for political communication. Appearing alongside Elon Musk, the visionary billionaire, has many messages: firstly, it gives Ron DeSantis national stature. Emmanuel Macron himself met Elon Musk during his official visit to the United States in December 2022. DeSantis attempts to symbolize that he thus fits into this category of statesmen and shows that he can work hand in hand with major business leaders. Secondly, it means that the two men agree on their rejection of the mainstream media and their respect for the First Amendment to the U.S. Constitution. Elon Musk is a provocative libertarian who likes to push the limits of free speech. He even invited Donald Trump to return to Twitter in November 2022, but Trump declined. DeSantis is also very attached to the First Amendment and a literal interpretation of the Constitution. And so, although they come from different political backgrounds, DeSantis and Musk are both advocates of freedom of expression. Only time will tell if this is just a casual alliance, or if it represents the beginnings of a common doctrine, or even of Conservatism 2.0.

CONCLUSION

DeSantis the protector, DeSantis the fighter, DeSantis the brave.

DeSantis the conservative, DeSantis the arrogant, DeSantis the aggressive.

Depending on the media, two images of the same man clash. In 2022–2023, his image was being worked on to win over Republican voters. The stakes were high because whoever made it through to the final duel, the face-off with the Democrat candidate, had every chance of becoming the next president of the United States. The battlefield of the Republican primaries was rich in Republican candidates, but Ron DeSantis couldn't defeat Donald Trump. The open war against his former mentor was hard-fought and commented, which is something the Biden camp was looking forward to.

DeSantis is consistent in his guiding principles: Christian, anti-establishment, anti-federal government. He defends the interests of the middle class. He has done a great deal for education in Florida, a territory usually reserved for Democrats. He also focuses on law enforcement. The aim is to position himself as the spearhead of Law and Order, promising more resources for police forces and for the fight against liberal judicial reforms.[1] He cultivates an image of incorruptibility. Recall that he refused all types of benefits in kind, pension, and health insurance when he arrived as a young representative in the Washington House in January 2013. Incidentally, his personal fortune is estimated at $320,000 in June 2022 according to Celebrity Net Worth, which is modest for a politician of his caliber. His wife Casey and three young children contribute to his image as a honest, hard-working family man.

---

1 Jonathan Weisman and Emma G. Fitzsimmons, DeSantis Visits 3 States on Tour Meant to Show He Is Tough on Crime, *The New York Times*, February 22, 2023.

Before dropping out of the presidential race and endorsing Trump, DeSantis said in a video posted shortly before the Iowa caucuses on January 15, 2024[2]: "Donald Trump is running for his issues, Nikki Haley is running for her donors' issues, I'm running for your issues, your family's issues, and solely to turn this country around." He also added: "I'm the only one that's beaten the left on issue, after issue, after issue." He will surely have left his mark, but his campaign was a balancing act that failed to produce results in 2024.

The primaries system is such that Donald Trump is in good position to win the party's nomination. However, legal scholars, national security experts, and political analysts[3] agree on the high uncertainty around this very particular election.[4] In a potential Trump Administration II, everything is possible, and time will tell how DeSantis can eventually reconnect with Trump, shall he wish to do so.

In politics, the wheels turn quickly. DeSantis could have an appointment with history in 2028 shall he decide to run again. But whatever happens next for him, he will have set the course for the rest of his promising career and will have marked his era. The Florida model is inspiring many Republican governors and legislators, who are beginning to apply the same methods and toolbox in their states, changing the lives of millions of Americans beyond Florida. DeSantis will also have focused the 2024 presidential election campaign on the culture war and immigration issues, rather than on taxes or the economy. By doing so, he provided the Republican Party with new battle horses that differentiate them from the Democrats, as they pursue a relatively protectionist economic policy that is ultimately little contested among Republicans.

"Freedom is never more than one generation from extinction," said Ronald Reagan in a 1964 speech. DeSantis's declared mission is a promise to give the United States and Americans their freedom back.

Freedom takes on different contours for every one of us. Freedom to choose our sexual orientation, our religion, our dress code, our lifestyle. Freedom for women to choose whether or not to have children. Freedom to raise these

---

2 Jeongyoon Han, Florida Gov. Ron DeSantis drops out of the presidential race, endorses Trump, *NPR*, January 21, 2024.

3 Politico Magazine, Supreme Court Shocker? Here's What Happens if Trump Gets Kicked Off the Ballot, *Politico*, February 5, 2024.

4 Ruth Igielnik and Andrew Fischer, Polls Have Shown DeSantis Trailing Trump, *The New York Times*, May 24, 2023.

children in accordance with one's values and faith. Freedom to bear arms or not. Freedom of expression.

Freedom is cherished by every American, but freedom is protean. Defining a common ground that works for all will be the challenge for the next generation of American politicians.

Printed in the USA
CPSIA information can be obtained
at www.ICGtesting.com
JSHW021629240324
59808JS00001B/1

9 781839 992049